PRAISE FOR AN EPIC U

"In his black T-shirts, Ali has given traditional bankers in their blue suits a run for their money. Hero."

Jort Kelder, journalist

"bunq always delights me with how intuitive yet innovative it is. So it is inspiring to find out the story behind this idealistic start-up unicorn."

Boris Veldhuijzen van Zanten, founder TNW

"Success favors the audacious."

Ilse Kamps, former CEO Catawiki and executive Booking.com

"Break Through Banking proves that you can contribute to a better world and build a successful business at the same time."

Steven Schuurman, founder Elastic

SIEBE HUIZINGA

Break Through Banking

kompas

Translation Cézanne Tegelberg / Lennard van Ree
Editor Toon van de Put
Cover Edoardo Mercati
Lay-out Iris Borst, i-design
Promotion and publicity Bert Gelderblom
Printed by Wilco BV
First edition 2017
Second renewed edition 2022

ISBN 978-94-92107-39-8

www.uitgeverijkompas.nl

'Fueled with ambition, we are bent on writing history. This could be your chance to be part of a game changing initiative – if you are up for it!'

— bunq —

Contents

Pure Inspiration

Joris Luyendijk

It's been five years since I immersed myself in the world of mega-banks for my book, *Swimming with Sharks.* My conclusion was that not much had changed since the 2008 crash, far from it even. Incredibly, it's been "business as usual".

Then one day Ali called me. Apparently he'd been looking at the crisis from a very different angle for the past few years by setting up an entirely new kind of bank. A real 'Silicon Valley'-like start-up, without the comfort of the sunny weather of California, located in an old vacated office building in the cold windy suburbs of Amsterdam.

bunq is no typical bank run by middle-aged men in expensive suits who make their money by taking risks with your money. It's quite the opposite. bunq is a club full of young pups in their twenties, dragged and lured to Amsterdam from all over the world, taken by Ali's charisma and his plan. To use new technology and start a bank that doesn't take risks by piggybacking on your money. A bank that makes its earnings simply by providing an excellent service to its clients. Is that even possible? In a tiny country like the Netherlands? Before the big boys in the USA beat them to it?

Yes, as it turns out, it is. And this book will tell you how and why. It's a story about hard-won victories over supervisors and red tape. About breakthroughs and setbacks, personal dramas, arguments and reconciliations. Real stamina and the guts to start over again and again. It's the romance of a start-up, but also the tragedy of compromise and grudging acceptance that the world can only move so fast. And it's a surprising story. Because who would have thought that the first challenger of the dinosaur banks would see the light of day thanks to a loan from... the ING bank!

We're at the start of a revolutionary age, similar to the 90s, when the first mobile phones popped up. Within a decade those first simple 'bricks' quickly evolved into the hypermodern and user-friendly iPhone 7 or Galaxy 8. 'The big banks are scared to death of people like Ali' said Jeroen Smit, author and expert in banking and innovation, during a Dutch television interview. Or, as a London-based banking expert put it: 'The question isn't whether IT companies will take over the banking world, it's when.' Ali's pack is spearheading this revolution. Their story is pure inspiration for those daring to believe in a positive future: about a pack of pups in Amsterdam who relentlessly hounded their dreams into reality.

THE DREAM

Money Dealers

'Banks,' says Ali, 'are money machines. They attract money at the cheapest possible rate, then go on and sell it for as much as they can. It's buy-and-sell, just like your local car dealer. A car dealer promotes his cars by claiming how reliable they are. Somehow, a car has always been owned by an old lady that only used it for her weekly shopping trips. Bankers are barely any different. They too sell reliability by claiming how secure and service-oriented they are. No matter what happens – or so they claim – they're going to be there for us. In reality however, banks have long since stopped being financial service providers. Instead, they have become money dealers. They no longer aim for profits gained as a result of satisfied clients, but instead opt for profit no matter what.'

Ali shoots a glance at Duke, one of his advisers at TransIP – a web hosting company he set up as a twenty-year-old during his university years. In just a few years he expanded it into the largest web-hosting provider of the Netherlands. With around 100 employees and over 200,000 clients, it has a turnover of tens of millions of euros.

Sitting across from each other at a restaurant, they appear to be polar opposites. He, Duke, is of robust build. With his dark-blond hair and cool blue gaze, he looks like the archetype of Dutch sobriety. He gives his full attention to his environment. Ali, boyish, has pitch-black hair and dark, flitting eyes. Hyperactive and constantly multitasking, he is easily distracted. His thoughts always a few steps ahead of the moment.

Their backgrounds are miles apart too. Duke, 43 years old, built his career within the corporate structures of the financial world, moving from company to company. Ali, fourteen years younger, is the self-made man. The non-conformist buccaneer, fan of Nietzsche and Dostoevsky. He prefers building his own corporate structures.

Despite their differences, they share important values and traits. Honesty and an open mind being the two main ones. Without these similarities they would never have connected.

Ali only accepts advice from people he likes and who tell him the truth. Why waste precious time on people who annoy you, or convey cryptic or inaccurate messages? If Ali likes you, and the feeling is mutual, then it must be because you have an open mind, an absolute precondition of innovation in Ali's eyes: 'only open minds can shape the future'.

'All this crap with bonuses and banks going under? It's all because of this trade-driven mindset of the past few decades. There was a time when banks were our partners. Their service actually contributed to our growth and welfare. The size of their trade — and with that their profit — was balanced out by the social landscape and kept in control by limitations of the available technology. The improvements in that technology removed barriers and unlocked a potential of endless profits. To achieve those profits, increasingly complex mathematical and interest models were created — foregoing client interests and disrupting the once healthy balance. And so while the profits increased, so did the risks. We've gotten to the point where banks spend most of their time sustaining themselves and thereby sustaining the problems they create. They've turned inward, into their own world, their own culture. Their primary objective merely being to survive instead of adding value. Once there was a point to banks — but now they have turned into unbound profit-minded machines. The most important question is therefore: what's the next step forward?'

Duke listens carefully to what Ali has to say. He's heard him criticize banks before, but never in such a clear and sharp argument. Ali's obviously going somewhere with this...

Ali gauges Duke's reaction. He wants to know what he thinks of this new idea: the idea of an innovative, IT-driven bank; a radically renewed bank of the future, spawned from irritation of the existing banking system's self-serving efforts to prop up an outdated money industry.

Ali's irritation reached an all-time high a few weeks ago. On a beautiful summer day, during a small picnic, he received a phone call. TransIP was suffering and literally couldn't do any business because one of the primary online payment systems in the Netherlands was down. At that moment, a snippet from something he heard on the radio earlier that morning came to mind. The crisis was in full swing and politicians were scrambling over one another to spew their opinions on the matter. He realized there was something he could do. Why not overturn the banks' entire moneymaking system? Why not replace a complex structure made of cards, machines and bank transactions with a simple and direct payment system among people? Hadn't the start of TransIP once been brought on by his annoyance at the amount of paperwork and hand-filled forms that needed to be faxed over, just to register a domain name? The technology to deliver such huge change was already available and the need for change was massive.

And Duke? He has the financial background as well as the interest and intellect to not only grasp the idea, but also its consequences.

Duke refrains from answering and waits for Ali to recollect his thoughts. In the meantime, the latter replies to a message that popped up on his iPhone. The constant stream of messages on his phone seems never ending...

'Why not a bank that doesn't depend on interest revenue and complicated, risky business models,' Ali continues. 'A bank that transfers your money directly, without first parking it on a massive account just to make even more money. A bank that would have far fewer risks, it wouldn't be "too big to fail" or "too complex to grasp". Nor would you need a deposit guarantee scheme. And society wouldn't end up paying the price if it failed. Wouldn't it be great if you could change the essence of banking? If you turned it back from a money-dealer to a service organization? When you change the essence, the rest automatically falls into place. What would that look like? Like a small IT and service providing organization with an app, a website and a database. It would be a simple platform, not a huge collection of buildings. *Wikipedia* instead of the *Encyclopedia Britannica*. Would you still use nickel, cotton fiber and plastic for your payments? Would you still have to line up at a bank counter between nine and five? No, of course not. No piles of credit and debit cards, no banknotes pulled from the wall like vending machines. Payments would no longer be in cash, complicated and expensive, but simple, safe and fast. How great would it be if money itself became pure again? If it became a social binding agent between friends, family and colleagues. If it were to be your money again, to do with as you please.'

'What about existing apps?' says Duke. 'Mobile banking, as banks offer it now?'

'Those apps are already completely obsolete. They do nothing more than just provide access to the outdated databases at larger banks. They don't contribute to the fundamental change to the system. Our app would work outside that system. We would offer high quality services and beautiful products, resulting in satisfied clients, thereby leading to profit. We would charge a simple subscription fee for the services and products provided. This allows us to not have to make up all sorts of derivatives. People are perfectly capable of managing their own money and no one needs a bank that's only interested in pushing more of its own products. And so,' Ali summarizes the idea, 'we develop a service organization for payments, no more and no less. A social network for payments, bypassing old-fashioned banks. A network that surpasses big banks in terms of day-to-day money needs, and changes the world. We're going to shake things up and give people back what they're entitled to: control over their own money. What do you think?'

Duke has a moment of silence. He sips his coffee and gazes out the window. He realizes that Ali's question is no innocent one. In reality it means: are you in? Ali needs someone who knows his way around the financial world, someone like him. Together they would make a great team indeed. A positive answer would however also imply his departure from the comfort of Ernst & Young, where he was recently promoted to Executive Director of Transaction Advisory Services.

'All this commotion over bonuses and bankrupted banks,' Duke inquires, searching for a decision, 'where do you think it stems from? They're not the only companies to go bankrupt, and performance-related pay exists everywhere. Why are so many people anti-bank? Are banks really that bad?'

'No, banks are neither good nor bad,' answers Ali. 'And although many call bankers unethical moneygrubbers, I don't have any negative feelings towards them. Some of my old classmates ended up working for banks. They weren't unethical at all. They just ended up working for companies in a dysfunctional system. The core problem is this mindset of infinite money-dealing, which inevitably causes financial gluttony, leading to unacceptable risks.'

Duke nods. It's not the bankers, not the employees, it's the consequence of an obsolete system... 'I'll consider it,' he says.

Ali pays the bill. As they exit the restaurant, the sparrows scatter from their path. Duke heads to his semi-electric bicycle at the north exit of the Max Euweplein, a square in Amsterdam. 'Homo sapiens non urinat in ventum' is inscribed across the archway: 'Sensible people don't pee into the wind'.

Duke absentmindedly fidgets with the lock. A new sort of bank, an app really, nothing more... *What do you think? What's the next step forward?*

As he rides his bike through the beautiful streets of Amsterdam, his mind keeps going over their conversation. Memories of his time at Citibank start to loom. It was over ten years ago: he spent each and every day optimizing yield to maximize profits. In the morning, the money flowed in, often several billions. By the evening it was gone again. Yet somehow more than enough money was left each day to cover for the office space, the employees and the shareholders. Everyone had their own task to keep the system going, but no one seemed to consider what they were actually doing anymore. Most of them were primarily concerned with reeling in their bonuses, while others focused on backstabbing their colleagues.

It all boils down to what's the right thing to do? And how do we make this come true? This idea completely changes the view of what a bank should be. What if we really could change the system? What if — even in a minor way — we could actually change that essence and transform it into something new? If we could do more than just keep talking about change and complain about all that is wrong with the world? Would our efforts mean that we could actually change the world for the better? Slowly but surely a feeling creeps up on him: maybe, just maybe, change would be possible. Maybe they really can make a difference.

Lost in his thoughts, Duke doesn't hear the frantic ringing of the tram until the very last moment. He immediately hurls himself and his bike out of the tram's path, barely avoiding a grim collision. His rear tire gets caught in the tracks. He manages to pull away in the nick of time, just in front of the oncoming wheels.

He texts Ali: 'Your plan is mind-boggling: I nearly got

hit by a tram...'

Sensible or not, he realizes: they shall be peeing into the wind.

Today marks July 19, 2012.

Banking Debt

In 2012, the Netherlands spends its fourth year in crisis. The housing market has stagnated, the construction industry is lying idle, companies have stopped investing in practically anything and the number of bankruptcies has risen yet again. Unemployment hasn't been this high in years. Over half a million people are jobless; 7 percent of the total workforce. There is even mention of the largest economic crisis since 1930. And the financial sector is the one to blame, with banks taking the lead.

'Too big to fail' was the term the American government used to describe the banking sector when collective bankruptcy loomed four years ago. Since 2002, the US had been developing a habit of giving out mortgages to anyone who wanted one. 'We want everybody in America to own their own home. That's what we want,' president George Bush Jr had said during a speech at Washington University. And the financial world gladly obliged. They offered an increasing number of mortgages to people that could not sustain them because of existing debts or other kinds of high-risk profiles. Thanks to a range of fiscal tricks, this went well for a number of years and the mortgage market grew to monstrous proportions. Until 2007, when an increasing number of Americans were unable to pay their – at times even quintuple – mortgages. Inflation was up and the variable mortgage interest rates went up along with it. The monthly costs quickly became unbearable for more and more homeowners forcing them to sell and leave their houses. But there was no one left to sell their properties to.

Overnight, the big mortgage providers ended up in big trouble. With increasingly complex financial products, they had built enormous golden castles. But when the foundation, the housing and the mortgage market, began to crumble, the castles started to collapse one by one. The financial models proved useless and resulted in losses of billions of dollars and in bankruptcies. Because the rating agencies – assigned with the task of determining the quality of financial products – were (purposely or not) completely off the mark, banks no longer dared to lend each other money. The entire financial system was hanging by a thread. Things were very close to becoming completely gridlocked – as they did in the 30s, which back then led to devastating results that have scarred history permanently. This time, the American government came to the rescue: they poured tens of billions of dollars worth of tax money into the system in order to keep things standing – succeeding by only a very small margin. The entanglement had become so great that even a single bankruptcy could tear the entire system down.

Things were quite similar in the Netherlands. The banking sector has grown to four times the size of the real economy. This size is built on the same financial houses of cards, and certainly not on traditional Dutch ruggedness. If banks would declare bankruptcy, it would be a disaster for society here too. Payments would stall, exchange of goods and services would cease. Investors and savers would lose their money, wages would go unpaid.

And so 'healthy and viable' banks and insurers could apply for 20 billion euros worth of support from the government. ING, Aegon and SNS Reaal, all far from healthy, gladly made use of the offer. Fortis/ABN Amro is already beyond rescue and is nationalized: more tax money is used to pay for it. This increases the already hefty public debt with an additional 30 billion euros, equating to over 4,000 euros per working Dutch citizen. Spread across all men, women and children, the rescue operation costs nearly 1,800 euros per person. Some time later it turns out that SNS is still unable to stand on its own feet. An additional 3.7 billion euros later, the bank is nationalized as well.

The credit crisis is also an image crisis, a moral crisis. Because it's not the financial system that bears the consequences of its own mismanagement, but society as a whole. It's not the perpetrators who are made to pay, but the victims. Are the banks and insurers themselves not also victims of the stagnated housing market and the failing economy? No. They're victims of their own non-transparent constructions. In pursuit of ever increasing profits, they've allowed themselves to become dependent on them, rendering their entire financial empire volatile.

Scandals fuel the increasing anger towards the banks: the Libor scandal comes to light at the end of 2008. It turns out that banks have been willfully manipulating the most important interest rates in the financial world, the 'London Interbank Offered Rate', or Libor. This is the interest rate banks charge when lending one another money. We're talking about tens of billions of euros per day, where even the smallest manipulation can lead to a huge amount of extra profit. And to top it all off, in the Netherlands the 'profiteering scandal' is exposed. Over seven million investments with a promised higher return were sold. However, due to hidden costs, they had barely created any value at all. Even worse, they frequently result in losses. The scandal follows the revelation of equally misleading capital accelerators and profit triplers: stock rental agreements that promised profits, but instead led to huge and remaining debts.

Even now, banks and insurers show no interest in taking any responsibility. From 2008 onwards the executives continue to grant themselves their bonuses. They are forced to do so — or so they say — because their talents and responsibilities are so immense. But their responsibility for all that has gone wrong remains painfully unacknowledged. They are, after all, intelligent men — and the odd women — who are very capable of rationalizing both their behavior as well as their actions. Capable of proving the benefits of their function within the system and receiving the necessary recognition and confirmation from those around them. Incapable, however, of admitting their accountability or taking the blame: not because they choose not to, but because they neither see, nor experience their faults. Ironically, they are the only ones not carrying the debt of the banks: financially or morally.

Nothing changes. Banks continue to take unpredictable risks, charge high costs, pay out ridiculous bonuses and let the clients and society pay the debt whenever their gambling greed turns out for the worse. Their financing is expensive and their loans come with ambiguous conditions. It's completely opaque how the level of interest is determined and unclear how a bank invests your money. What is clear, is that you have very little choice in the matter.

Moral appeal and regulation don't stand a chance against such a fortress. It's the outsiders, the newcomers, who will have to come up with new alternatives. They will have to make the financial world change.

But how do you break through these banks?

Project Clear

For the first few months, Duke and Ali meet for a few hours a week, in evenings and on weekends. They discuss the ideal organization, its structure and culture and how to gear up for a revolution. A revolution, says Ali, is to give people back the power over their money. To do so, they plan to take on one of the most powerful industries in the world: the banking industry.

Duke suggests a name: 'Project Clear'. 'Clear' refers to transparency and 'clearing': the processing of payments between financial institutions. Beyond that, it reveals little.

Project Clear, they decide, should be a flat organization: young, driven and informal, limiting formalities to the bare minimum. It should also be a small, tight-knit group: innovative and revolutionary. Of course there will be teams and specialisms, but no red tape or partition walls. The gang of rebels will consist of the best of the best in IT, marketing, and financial and legal affairs. They will mainly look for young people, in their early twenties, without experience in the banking world. Money must not be their primary incentive. Duke and Ali want fresh ideas and as little contamination from the world of banking as possible.

Duke brings financial and banking expertise to the table, plus a sizable network. He will be taking care of the financing via TransIP. He will say goodbye to his prerogatives at EY. Ali, who as owner/director lives and breathes TransIP seven days a week, wants to free up three to four days for Project Clear. He will focus his attention on the development of software and finding coders: the programmers who will be writing that software.

In order to be able to develop the ideal bank, Ali notes, they will need to be autonomous. Only then can they operate the way they want to. As long as the payments run through other banks, they will have no control over them, making it impossible for them to execute their ideas fully. That would result in being a simple middleman, a payment service like any other. Also, Ali fears that their entire business concept will fall apart if they make themselves dependent on the fees the banks charge. Those fees have already been proven to fluctuate; for instance the banks simply increased their interest rate spreads the last time it suited them. With their own banking permit from The Central Bank of the Netherlands ('De Nederlandsche Bank', or DNB in short), Project Clear will be in charge of their own turf.

According to the Act on Financial Supervision, the equity capital of a bank must be at least five million euros. The quality of coding is their greatest asset as well as their largest expense. It will form the foundation of innovation, their IT-driven bank. Everything around it, the entire organization they dream of, is just facilitatory. Their company needs to shape up in six months to a year, with a marketing budget from the halfway-point to generate publicity for Project Clear. After the start-up phase, revenue will begin to flow in: an x amount of users, business and private, paying an x amount of euros in service costs.

They estimate the required five million to be more than enough to cover their simple activities. Okay, there's always the risk of things overrunning in time or cost, so add a million to be sure: five to six, then. If they do run into unforeseen costs or losses, those will be covered by TransIP, or in other words: by Ali.

Ali's going all-in; he's willing to invest all of his money — and more, if necessary. He doesn't have to start from scratch, as he did with TransIP, but whatever the cost: the bank of the future shall exist!

With the outlines of Project Clear sketched out, they can begin to fill in the blanks. For the early start-up phase, they need people with different skills and common analytical vigilance, who will be able to oversee the possibilities, difficulties and effects of the new bank in the making. They need to get things on track, fast.

At 8 pm on a Wednesday, Attila's phone rings. He is a programmer at Capgemini, in his mid-twenties, wears glasses and has a receding ginger hairline. His eyebrows are the same color, giving his face a rusty look. Before he started working as a programmer, he studied artificial intelligence and computer systems that display a form of 'thinking', or intelligent behavior. The definition is not very precise, as the concept of 'intelligence' is similarly indistinct.

On the other end of the phone is Ali. Attila's already heard of him through a friend at TransIP: 'He's looking for coders'. They arrange to meet that same evening at half past nine in Café Thijssen, on the corner of the Lindengracht and the Brouwersgracht in Amsterdam.

At Café Thijssen, Attila signs the non-disclosure agreement, after which Ali lays his cards on the table. It sounds like a dream to Attila: helping to build a system that will create a whole new manner for people to handle their money through their smartphones. A system is already beginning to unfold in his mind, branching out like a social network.

That night Attila can't sleep. He enjoys his current job and it offers him comfort and security, but he also sees the unique nature of the opportunity in front of him. His decision the next morning is crystal clear and final: after his planned holiday, he will leave Capgemini.

Two weeks later, Attila is the first employee on the payroll. In fact, he's so early that there's not even an office yet. There is, however, a website. A very simple one saying:

> Project Clear is an Amsterdam-based international start-up, backed by one of the most successful young entrepreneurs from the Netherlands. As a company we are building an efficient and scalable platform from scratch. Perfection is the standard. The atmosphere, however, is informal and relaxed. Everyone feels responsible for success, with a high level of autonomy. Due to the impact of the project, we cannot disclose more info without an NDA.
>
> Curious? Please send your resume and code to gogogo@projectclear.nl.

Meanwhile, Duke has introduced Ron, an old friend of his, who can help quantify the project's expense. He has experience in the banking world – not necessarily an advantage in Ali's opinion. But it has been a while since his banking days, and Ali – against his nature – compromises.

Duke's brother Pjotr also comes aboard. He's an engineer in bioinformatics, a field that uses supercomputers to analyze biological data. It's thanks to this that the human genome was mapped. Pjotr will co-code and lead the IT guys.

The third person Duke brings in is Long, a former intern at EY, of Chinese origin. He's an econometrician who works magic with mathematical models. In his spare time, he plays guitar with his friends outside a supermarket entrance.

All three of them sign the non-disclosure agreement. Nothing of what they're about to do must leak out.

Office space is the next step. Early December they find something suitable along the Arlandaweg, a thoroughfare in Amsterdam Sloterdijk. It's part of the linear and bewildering road network surrounding the train- and metro station, which has been under a constant state of reconstruction for years. Cars drive too fast, and even the wind finds shortcuts between the tower block office buildings. It's a deserted and disheveled place — perfectly suited for the covert operation they're about to pursue.

And so they move in. On the second floor of one of these towers, two little electric heaters are blowing out hot air at the top of their lungs. They give off just enough heat to keep out a bit of the cold and dampness, but they're nowhere near powerful enough to provide any real comfort. Mondays are the worst. The first few hours are arctic. Adding heaters is impossible; the wiring in the building is gray with age and fraying at the edges. Any attempt at turning up the heat leads to glowing copper and smoldering plastic.

Attila simply always keeps his coat on. He's working on the first steps towards a user-friendly and playful app, and a safe and efficient payment platform: making demos and performing tests on smartphones.

He programs in PHP, a much-used and tested scripting language. In the computing world however, another language is trending at that time: Scala. Some programming errors show up more easily in Scala. The coding itself, however, is way slower compared to PHP.

Pjotr, responsible for IT, chooses to go with Scala. Attila will need to learn this coding language first, and flies to London for a two-day workshop.

As soon as he returns, Attila receives backup from Peter, an American. This hardened hedonist from New York City has a broad field of interest. Although he studied political science, he prefers coding. He's one of the smartest around, but by no means one of the slimmest. Apart from well-functioning programs, he also builds well-filled sandwiches: two slices of ham, three layers of salami, cheese to taste and a homemade dressing on top.

The basic idea behind this collaboration is that a coder needs to be able to work both at the front and back-end of the program. The user side is the front: the app you see on your smartphone or tablet. In order to design it, you need to be able to get into the mind of the user. See what they see and imagine how they'll want to use it. Following that, you have to be able to code in such a way that you make the desired image technically possible. In the back-end, outside of the user's view, the app communicates with the payment software on the server. That's where the actual data is stored and worked with. Changes in the app have consequences for the server software and vice versa.

The main language in the office is English, not only out of courtesy to Peter. The fact that Ali's company TransIP was started up as a Dutch company held it back in its natural cross-border growth. The focus on the Netherlands turned out to be a limitation that barely allowed TransIP to gain ground in Spain, for example. Without an international identity and orientation, you always need some form of representation abroad, a go-between. This structural flaw in DNA robbed TransIP of the possibility to grow into a world player. Ali calls it the greatest tragedy he ever inflicted on his company.

Never again. Project Clear must expand to international success. The revolution has to be able to catch on, start in Europe, then move across the continent to Asia and, possibly, even Africa. Project Clear also wants to be able to attract coders from all over the world. Only then will it get the very best people. In short: with English as a main language, Project Clear prevents any form of isolation from the rest of the world.

Duke and Ali, with all their differences and similarities, have never worked together as intensively as this. From an empty office, rented out to them under an ad hoc guardian scheme to keep out squatters, they will be changing the world. But even the most inspiring movements are not immune to differences in opinions — especially not from within.

After planning the revolution, Duke and Ali have different paths in mind. They agree that acquiring a bank status is important in order to make Project Clear into a true bank of the future. But is it a prerequisite?

Duke knows that obtaining a permit required for the bank status is practically impossible and hasn't been done in decades, especially not by a greenfield player. In Duke's view, Ali's drive, impatience and confidence is making him underestimate the effort that acquiring this permit will take.

Ali, in turn, marks Duke's 'realism' as 'yes-but behavior'. It makes him even more eager to proceed. He sees realism as a lack of imagination and courage, an excuse not to take any risks or show full commitment. Realizing a dream is unrealistic by definition. Besides, fear only leads to structural problems. 'Those who refuse to leave their caves, starve.'

Around Christmas time, Duke permanently moves in to the ice-cold Arlandaweg office. Christmas is the season of giving and should come with a gift, Ali decides, but what? He wants something with impact and meaning but also something that's affordable. A start-up should be frugal. After all, the one thing you can plan for is that nothing ever goes according to plan.

While mulling over an IT problem, an entrepreneurial classic comes to him. Quartz crystal, an essential component of computer chips, once lifted society to new heights by being used as flint stone. Exposing quartz crystals to an electric current makes them vibrate at a frequency of 32.768 Hz. This frequency is equal for all quartz crystals, anywhere in the world and even beyond.

Swiss watch manufacturer Girard Perregaux, in existence since 1791, invented quartz as an alternative for the hitherto mechanically driven movement. The surrounding clock manufacturers however, were too traditional to be open to change and chose not to adapt. The invention remained unused for years: too many vested interests still revolved around miniature cogs and windup springs.

In Japan however, things went very differently. Eight years after Perregaux, SEIKO decided to launch a quartz watch: the *Calibre 0614*, with a 6-digit Liquid Crystal Display. The neighboring companies immediately got on board, and twenty-six months later, the market share of the Swiss mechanical watch took a global tumble. It decayed at an incredible pace from a staggering 90% to a mere 10%.

Ali smiles. This story is their story: with a simple idea and technological innovation, they will challenge the established industry after decades of stagnation. In the same way the thought-to-be steadfast Swiss watch industry lost its footing, Project Clear will shake up the oligopoly of the banking world.

You can get a Casio F-91W quartz watch for as little as fifteen euros; the Christmas present has been found. From now on, every employee that makes it through their trial period will receive a Casio.

When handing over the watch, Ali explains that the Casio should be a constant reminder of how quickly a small change can wipe out a seemingly impenetrable market, by simply making use of the biggest mistake and worst habit of any established order: arrogance. Arrogance makes a person both lazy and blind.

The next day, Duke pops in on Ali, snickering: 'Did you choose this model on purpose?'

'Why? I explained the whole symbolism behind it, didn't I?'

'In Afghanistan, Al Qaida uses this exact model of Casio

watches to ignite roadside bombs.'

Ali clears his throat with a slight sense of discomfort.

Docter's Note

At the start of the new year the discussion about the banking permit flares up again. Duke and Ali agree conceptually, but Duke still has practical objections. Even with all the time, money and effort in the world, it's still very unlikely that DNB would ever grant them one. Since Triodos Bank – 'sustainable banking since 1980' – they haven't issued a single permit to a greenfield enterprise. Any party that did receive one after that time – online broker Binck, for example, and DSB by Dirk Scheringa – were already under the supervision of DNB and the AFM (Dutch Financial Authority) on account of previous permits. Knab bank is a branch of Aegon Bank. And to make things worse: the regulatory pressure due to more laws and other mandatory rules have increased tenfold since then.

A number of banks have gone bankrupt in the last few years and had to be saved by the state. Hence DNB will be very careful to avoid repetition. Especially with a newcomer, they will be reluctant to take on any risk. Especially when it belongs to one person: A. Niknam, a director/owner. After all, wasn't DSB a one-man bank too?

'We don't even like banks. Why press to become one?' asks Duke. 'It's much more realistic to start out as a payment service provider. Then, once we have a client base and we've proven ourselves, we apply for a permit and become a bank.'

For Ali, this is out of the question. However difficult or improbable the license seems: to him it is simply a prerequisite. He doesn't know how yet, but they will get one. If not from DNB, it'll have to be from a foreign supervisory body. The harmonization of European rules opens up that option. For now, he's sticking to his own motto: 'However absurd the ambition may be, be rigorous in its execution and things will work out in the end.'

What concerns Ali more is the dilemma they create by wanting to obtain a banking license. Should Project Clear, an IT initiative, conform to the same rules, conditions and structures as banks that represent the 'old world'? Does that not cause a conflict between the informal culture they want and the formal structures they would have to adhere to? Will they be able to keep up their pace and efficiency? There is a massive gap between what they want to be and what they have to do to become it. To what extent, Ali wonders, are they about to sell their soul?

They will need to surround that soul with two necessary and compulsory bodies: a Board of Directors and a Supervisory Board. The management, or Board of Directors, is roughly outlined already. Duke is the COO, Chief Operational Officer, Ali the CEO, Chief Executive Officer. The third compulsory post of CFRO, Chief Financial & Risk Officer, is still open.

The Supervisory Board, responsible for overseeing the management internally, is a different story. It needs to be composed of respected and confidence-inspiring individuals from the financial world. Although such a board usually operates at a distance and only as a formality, Duke and Ali actually want it to be of practical use to them. Neither of them actually know how an application for a permit works and how to increase their chances of success. A capable commissioner could help them with that. The perfect candidate would know the way in with the supervisor and open doors that would otherwise remain closed. Also, he or she would provide Project Clear with a certain level of credibility and serve as a sounding board.

They compile a shortlist. At the top there is a name of fame: Arthur Docters van Leeuwen, jurist and senior civil servant.

Docters van Leeuwen was born in The Hague, shortly after the Dutch Famine of World War 2 ('Winter of Hunger'), on May 8, 1945, the last day of the food drops over the Duindigt racetracks. This exceptionally intelligent character with the marked appearance of an English bulldog was, among others, inspector of State Funds, head of the Dutch Secret Service (now the AIVD) and Chairman of the Board of Procurators General in The Hague. Also, he spent a number of years as chairman of the AFM. Although he is no longer at the center of attention, he is still a significant financial authority, known for his intellect and no-nonsense vision.

Project Clear has much to gain from a commissioner of his stature. His massive network, enormous knowledge of banks and his access to the financial world would make obtaining a banking license a lot more realistic. But what's in it for him? Why would someone with such a track record commit himself to a start-up by two financial nobodies? Even in the autumn of someone's career, an adventure like that is a huge risk. These are questions only their dream commissioner Docters van Leeuwen himself can answer. And so they embark on a search, hoping to share their dream with him.

Duke and Ali phone and email friends, colleagues and acquaintances in order to get in touch with Docters van Leeuwen's acquaintances, colleagues and friends. Halfway through January, they strike gold. They get a very meaningful email in 007 style:

> Got info directly from contacts inside the secret service. Pet name for secret agent 001 is Thure. Beware: the line is tapped. ;-)

Also, a former colleague from the AFM days is willing to give Docters van Leeuwen a call and introduce Duke and Ali in advance. When it comes to Project Clear however, they'll have to do their own convincing.

For three nights, Ali and Duke write, re-write and re-word their letter:

> Dear Mr. Docters van Leeuwen,
>
> (...) Project Clear started earlier this year to establish a new player in the European financial market. Equipped with a strong team, we are looking to reform the current way of doing things. Because of the financial crisis and SEPA (Single Euro Payments Area) the time is right for the use of technology to give clients the power over their own money. In doing so we take the point of view of the client and society as opposed to being stuck to existing systems and products. You will understand that this is a fundamental paradigm shift and that it will drive changes necessary in the financial industry.

> The first step is a highly efficient financial platform, enabling a new business model for payment transactions and financial services. We would very much like to give you a short demonstration of a solution we have created in this short period of time. Subsequently, we are eager to discuss the business model and the philosophy behind it with you, and ask for your opinion on our venture.
>
> Sincerely.

The envelope also contains the book that Ali wrote about his experiences with TransIP: *Entrepreneurs never catch a break.*

A few days later, Ali is rushing along the A44 from Amsterdam to TransIP in Leiden, annoyed as usual at the slow traffic around him. He calls Duke for a daily update. The latter's 'hey' is of a higher pitch and longer duration than usual: more like 'hurray!'

'What's up?' Ali asks.

'We have an answer already! Docters van Leeuwen is coming over! In little over a month, on February 16!'

Ali is glowing with triumph. The fact that someone like Docters van Leeuwen would respond within a week and initiate his own visit is an acknowledgement that their idea, however minimally described in their letter, is of actual significance.

In thirty days, everything needs to be in shape. The app is still useless, the business plan filled with cracks and the 'strong team' with which they 'are working to establish a new player in the European financial market' still only consists of five guys in a deserted office. They need to get to work immediately. Ali hits the gas and his car leaps forward.

'We're starting a bank,' says Duke.

Daan, 28 years old, frowns with disappointment. He knows Duke from EY where they worked together. He already picked up on something brewing at Ali's birthday party. 'It's huge', Ali had said back then.

Daan presses his lips together and the corners of his mouth drop. 'A... bank?'

During his international business economics studies, he promised himself never to apply for a job at a bank. He's not into suits and black shoes. It would be like working in a crematorium that burns other people's money. For five years at EY he occupied himself with analyses, business models, mergers and take-overs. Every year, the novelty wore off faster. Especially mergers and take-overs had turned into a game that, to be honest, had started to bore Daan.

His breaking point was a job for SNS Property Finance, the wavering real estate branch at SNS Reaal Bank which was likely to be nationalized, and later in fact did get nationalized at the expense of 3.6 billion euros. He was asked to compile data on property values and financing into a model and co-write a report. Although it seemed as if the client himself hadn't the first clue about numbers, it became obvious that the report was to stick to the facts as perceived by the client, as opposed to reality.

It was obvious to Daan: this was not the place for him. He was in the process of scanning through job vacancies when Duke left unexpectedly – and now, they were calling him.

Having snuck out of the office with an excuse, dressed in his Oger suit, no tie, Daan is sat in one of the second hand desk chairs, across from Duke. The non-disclosure agreement he signed didn't contain any deal breakers. And he trusts Duke and Ali. But... *a bank*?

Daan's discomfort dissipates when Ali joins them at the table and brings up the subscription model. 'The client only pays a certain amount for a simple service,' Ali explains. 'That service is no more than a mobile bank account with a fully mobile payment method. We only make money if we actually provide something.'

'The license application will be completed halfway through February, and we'll be going live at the end of May,' Duke concludes.

That very weekend, Daan discusses the terms of his contract with Duke and quits his job at EY. Thanks to a reservoir of annual leave and a record-time job handover, he starts work at Arlandaweg the following Monday. His suit stays in the closet at home and his lease car replaced by a tram. He's carrying a heavy desktop computer in a supermarket shopping bag. Providing a fully functioning workspace was his own responsibility.

Daan is going to put Project Clear's business model back on track. This was Ron's job, but as rigorously as Daan has left EY behind, Ron is leaving Project Clear. The contrast with his old banking environment is too big. Hugely interesting, these start-ups, but so young, informal, and 'messy'... It's not 'his thing'. Also, he doesn't think Project Clear is 'corporate' enough to be able to make the difference. His departure could leave a huge gap in terms of experience, but it doesn't seem to worry Ali. Ron has a background in banking. His departure doesn't just mean one less compromise, it also increases the chances of speeding things up. Besides, Daan's here now, right?

Essentially, the business model is very simple. Project Clear is an independent IT-driven service organization with revenue from subscriptions. Sending or receiving payments should be as easy as sending or receiving messages. Everything is automated and scalable, ensuring minimal costs. Its existence is justified only by satisfied customers. The intended clientele consists of supermarkets, cafés, online shops and other parties from mainly small and medium enterprises, for whom the system is a great advantage: a basic tablet can serve as a till, ready for use. Investing in expensive cash register systems and card terminal subscriptions would no longer be necessary.

Daan enters a cost prognosis into Excel, calculates the minimal number of subscribers needed to break even and assesses the feasibility of Project Clear. The subscriptions, however, which form the foundation of the business model, are a headache. Like Ron, Daan comes up with a multitude of subscription varieties, calculates them and throws them out. The route to a solution is hidden inside a maze of detours.

Daan also throws himself on the financing challenge. The calculated five to six million is tight, and TransIP being the only source of finance is risky. Just because Ali's going all-in doesn't mean he has the required millions stashed under his mattress. Nor does TransIP have a huge balance sheet. If the project fails, there will be too little to gain for the men-in-suits. On the upside, TransIP has made a large profit for several years in a row. As a corporate finance specialist, Daan can see two options: financing based on future profit, or selling off TransIP.

The business model mentions looking for early adopters through social media. The first private subscribers need to start forming a critical mass, whereby their contact list is crucial. From their own phones, they can start to invite everyone they know to the payment service. In order to catch the attention of these frontrunners they need marketing — and fast.

'Walk with me,' Ali says to Djoeri, a 24-year-old TransIP employee. It's a Wednesday afternoon in the university city of Leiden. Djoeri gets up from his chair and follows Ali into 'Brazil': a cozy den with two leather sofas, floor lamps and a TV cabinet. It's directly to the left of the entrance, where TransIP receives new applicants: a psychoanalytical nook for scanning newcomers. The name is in line with 'Argentina', 'Chile', etc. It once sounded better than 'Room A' and 'Room C'.

Ali sees Djoeri as a 'diet version' of himself and Djoeri also considers the two of them to be more alike than he'd care to admit. Djoeri practically always understands what Ali means and how he thinks, provided the overall idea has been introduced to him beforehand. More importantly, he accepts Ali's brain-farts for what they are: facts-not-yet-realized. Subsequently, he does what he can to make them happen. However, where Ali is always very direct and resolute, Djoeri has a gentler side, he's more sensitive.

This makes him perfect for marketing and human resource tasks.

As soon as Djoeri shuts the door, Ali shoves the non-disclosure agreement under his nose.

'I'm working on something fucking awesome in Amsterdam. Sign here. Guess what I'm doing!' he asks, while Djoeri signs his name at the bottom of the document.

'Big data?'

'No. Starting a bank.'

It takes a moment to sink in.

'Have you completely lost your mind?! That's impossible!'

'My point exactly.'

Three days later, Djoeri makes his debut at Arlandaweg. Duke, Daan and Peter are sitting behind their computers in the large space, wearing their coats. Attila is typing away in an improvised office. Ali raises his voice for a moment. 'This is Djoeri. He's going to be taking care of marketing and HR, part-time. Like me, he'll be going back and forth between TransIP and here.'

It seems to be the right time for new initiatives like Project Clear. An online announcement appears for 'The Fifth Power: a different view on the news'. Rob Wijnberg, former editor in chief of established newspaper *NRC.next*, wants to create an ad-free news website that delivers journalistic items that go beyond day-to-day fads. 'How' and 'why' will be the leading questions. As soon as fifteen thousand people are willing to pay a sixty-euro subscription, it's on.

Ali sees a kindred spirit. An original view on things opens up new worlds, each offering countless possibilities.

He finds there to be a shocking lack of it, causing the world to advance at an irritatingly slow pace, and yes, even coming scarily close to a grinding halt. Also, Wijnberg undoubtedly has a strong network of colleagues and sympathizers. Good contacts in the media may come in handy in the future. It's never too early to consider such things.

There's another initiative, one receiving a great deal of press: the fast growth of sustainable supermarket chain Marqt. Ali already had his eye on Quirijn Bolle, founder of Marqt, before his conversation with Duke, to see if they might be able to help each other out. Emails had gone to and fro via mutual acquaintances to meet up sometime in September or October that year for a coffee at George, above the Marqt in Amsterdam's Utrechtsestraat. But Ali was either ill or TransIP was taking up a lot of his attention. Whatever the reason, the date passed and the coffee went cold. Ali's still disgruntled with himself for letting it slip by.

Bolle is all the more relevant to Duke, who is focusing more and more on business development. He wants to start by approaching supermarkets, festivals and parking services: organizations with a lot of (young) payment traffic. Their taking part in Project Clear would hugely boost their reach, and with that, their viability. If he wants to drop in on these potential partners, a flashy demo on his iPhone is crucial. After all, there is the hurdle of possibly-interested-parties having to sign a non-disclosure agreement before even sitting down with him. Why would they?

In view of Docters van Leeuwen's upcoming visit, spending half of his time working at Project Clear turns out to be too little for Ali. He's responsible for IT, the organization and the people, gets involved with marketing, and finds he has underestimated the amount of work and adversity he would have to face. At the same time, the hours he has left to spend on TransIP are nowhere near enough. The days are simply too short. Freeing up more time is impossible and his car's gas pedal has already reached its socially acceptable limit.

Ali doesn't blame this overload on his own underestimation, but on the slowness of all things physical. Nothing happens naturally, everything's a battle, and everything has to be overcome step by step. There's no precedent for what he's doing and Project Clear has only just begun.

Illustrative of his optimistic estimations of time is the promise he makes to Paul van Liempt, a journalist with a morning show on News Radio channel. They've known each other since the publication of Ali's book.

With his eye on Project Clear's nearby future, Ali has decided to make himself more visible to the outside world, albeit reluctantly. 'Exposure' may benefit a start-up, but not him personally: it invades his cherished anonymity and freedom.

In early February, he lets himself get roped into a radio debate held in a large theater in Amsterdam. The topic is Dutch entrepreneurship. Afterwards, he sends an email to the moderator, Van Liempt, because he wants to know what the latter thought of his media performance. He's concerned about coming across as tired, curt and inexperienced. Ali mentions that, given the impact of his new 'Project X', he may need to trade his comfortable backstage spot for a place in the spotlights. When the time comes, he wants to be vaguely comfortable on-camera.

Van Liempt reassures him. The performance was excellent: Ali had quickly gotten over his nerves and mingled in the conversation. His public announcement of refusing to employ more than forty-nine people, however, was unnecessary bravery. Van Liempt also recommends that Ali wears a jacket next time. However terrible that may sound, it simply creates a more serious impression — even on those who claim otherwise. He'd like to see Ali join the table again in a couple of months for the launch of 'Project X'.

Luckily, Van Liempt doesn't hold his breath.

Lion's Den

They worked late last night. The first ones didn't leave the office until 11 pm, two hours later than usual. In the afternoon, the software demo gave out. To make matters worse, the elevator refused to go either up or down for the umpteenth time this month. The landlord was hastily summoned, but this time the problem proved more than an easy fix. Everyone refused to leave the office before the problems were solved. Even the elevator engineer.

Their faces were tense. After all, the next morning was D-day: the day that Docters van Leeuwen would be dropping by. So as not to make the already muggy air in the office any stuffier, they ordered sushi instead of the usual Surinamese roti. It was quiet at the dining table. Everyone was deeply engaged in thought and quietly working on getting everything up and running again. The usually extremely laid-back elevator engineer was sweating like a pig, the smell of which slightly undermined their efforts.

Docters van Leeuwen's visit also occupies Ali's mind. He's never met the guard dog of the Dutch Financial system, but reckons he's a sharp-witted and original character. He's eager to meet him, and a little nervous. How should he present himself? Informal, as he is? No, that might appear too rude. But putting on a jacket, as Van Liempt advised him to do, seems a bit too much. He decides to be himself and address Docters van Leeuwen with 'u' (the Dutch formal pronoun for 'you'), a form of politeness he usually avoids because it creates too much emotional distance.

Although Docters van Leeuwen is now retired, there are absolutely no signs that he has entered the calm autumn of his life. He's working on two large advisory tasks: improving the supervision of legal advocacy and the reorganization of the Ministry of Foreign Affairs. Also, he is on various Supervisory Boards and he's just started writing a collection of poems.

Much has already been written about Docters van Leeuwen himself. In 2000, Ad van Liempt and Ger van Westing published *Stuck in a revolving door, Arthur Docters van Leeuwen and the Ministry of Justice 1995-1998*, and it was made into a television drama in 2003. It describes the clash between the 'crème de la crème of the Dutch state' (according to the Prime Minister at the time, Wim Kok) and Justice Minister Winnie Sorgdrager. The conflict led to Docters van Leeuwen's involuntary departure as Chairman of the Board of Procurators General, which in turn marked the beginning of his time at the AFM.

As soon as the bell rings, at precisely the agreed time, Duke rushes down the stairs. He opens the large, glass front door, welcomes Docters van Leeuwen and, without hesitation, invites him into the elevator.

Upstairs, Ali is waiting. He shakes Docters van Leeuwen's hand, which feels a little awkward and surreal. Because he knows the guard dog from television, half of his mind feels like it knows him. The other half realizes that they're complete strangers. Docters van Leeuwen, in turn, is instantly taken with Ali and doesn't feel at all as though they're meeting for the first time.

Anxiously, Duke and Ali show their guest around their

practically empty office; a few goal posts for games of anti-stress soccer break up the open space. On the wall, at a safe distance from the two dartboards, are two large prints by photographer-and-friend Pieter. The trance music which usually blares from the speakers has been turned down and the playlist has been adjusted to create the right vibe for the occasion. Ali nervously utters a few pleasantries while racking his brain, wondering to what extent a senior civil servant is used to the squalor of an anti-squat. Duke senses his infectious nerves, but manages to appear calm. They make their way to one of the paperboard rooms and shut the door.

Docters van Leeuwen sits down comfortably, leaning back in the chair offered to him. He waits for an opening move from either Duke or Ali. The movements of his head and hands are precise and gradual, without being slow. This control over his motor skills are the result of years of practice, aware of the effect it has on others. It has become such a part of himself that it marks his person.

Even more so than his body, his face displays self-control. He shows little to no emotion: doesn't smile to ease the other person's comfort, doesn't nod in agreement, nor frown in rejection. His silence and apparently withheld attitude invites the other to speak. Ali experiences it as though he is faced with an immeasurable intelligence, observing, scanning and weighing up the situation.

It's soon clear: Docters van Leeuwen is averse to casual conversation. Within a minute, and without much introductory babble, the moment arrives for Ali to propose the idea behind Project Clear. Ali's no fan of repetition. He fears that he won't be able to deliver their story with the same passion as he did the first few times. In his head, the idea has already become a fact and existing facts are bygones to him. But just for this moment, when he has to convince this great man, this authority, of their dream, he has to find a way to regain himself. He has to tap into that primary emotion, that full conviction of his own truth.

'The basic idea,' he begins, 'is to set up a service organization with a subscription model. Making-money-on-money is no longer sustainable for banks, which means existing systems and bank products have become outdated. Project Clear wants to be an IT company with a banking license and not a bank with an IT product. The difference between the two is the revenue model: an IT company makes money by providing a service. What we want...'

Docters van Leeuwen interrupts him. What does the revenue model look like? And the financing? He keeps throwing in short, direct questions about the points Ali is just about to expand on. What about the risks and the safety? The interventions interrupt the storyline, not so much to put Ali off his stride, but to get to the core quickly. Now and then, Ali pauses, glancing at Duke for support.

When Docters van Leeuwen has run out of questions, Ali uses his iPhone to demonstrate how payments can be made from one mobile device to another. And how, in the same way, they take place between a customer and a shopkeeper. Log in, choose a name from a contact list, transfer... The software demo, currently still less reliable than their elevator, runs like a charm.

'And what do you expect from me?' Docters van Leeuwen asks when Ali puts his phone down.

'We want to ask you to be chairman of the Supervisory

Board. To lend a critical view to what we're doing and advise us a few times a year.'

'Make no mistake,' Docters van Leeuwen responds, 'I'm not an easy guy. If I commit, I will actually check on you.'

'We wouldn't expect nor want any less,' they say.

Docters van Leeuwen folds his hands and leans back. 'The Persians,' he begins, with a reference to Ali's Iranian background, 'have been known for their techniques of temptation since ancient times. I came here today with the mere intention of satisfying my curiosity. But why beat about the bush when I already know the answer. You're authentic. Here's my first bit of advice: your anti-bank attitude is understandable, but inconvenient. I foresaw what you are doing now fifteen years ago. I am willing by definition and I'm in. Yes, I would be happy to chair your Supervisory Board.'

A perplexed silence follows. Duke and Ali barely dare to look at each other, that's how fragile the moment seems. One look, one word might interfere with the reality that's smiling at them so suddenly. *Docters van Leeuwen is in!*

They recover and regain their composure, and as though nothing of importance has happened, as though the world hasn't just turned its face towards the future, they continue to discuss operational and strategic affairs, such as other suitable commissioners. Ali decides to refrain from sharing his preference for DJ Armin van Buuren, for now.

For lunch they have grilled cheeses. Docters van Leeuwen accepts the invitation to join them. The youthful testosterone at the joint table leads the conversation onto women, an area where young men and old lions are evenly matched.

As he leaves, Docters van Leeuwen hands out a small pile of homework: they're to read two books, which he mentioned several times throughout the conversation: *Phases* by Bernard Lievegoed and *Discorsi* by Niccolò Machiavelli.

Phases makes a link between ambitions and the phases of life. Docters van Leeuwen says that, according to Lievegoed's theory, he himself is in a period that offers more space for passing on the wisdom of life. Ali is in the twenty-eight to thirty-five category: youth is over and the earnestness of life has definitively begun. You know what you're capable of, what you struggle with and what's unattainable. You're approaching the peak of your productivity.

The day ends with booze and creeps through the evening into night and then morning. About to roll into bed, and still euphoric, Ali posts on Facebook:

> Win! What a great guy! Wise, experienced, intelligent and empathic. Knowing Dostoevsky inside out and Raskolnikov's pitfalls. A significant day. Indescribable. My homework is to read Lievegoed. Will do so gladly. (...)

Docters van Leeuwen is fully convinced of the importance of Project Clear. Besides, it's a simple consideration. Accepting a commissariat or other type of job mostly depends on whether he detects a natural, personal mutual understanding. He does. The conversation was to the point, prompt and leaped ahead, without many oversights. Also, these are nice guys who have proven themselves already. And if he's misjudged them: shame, he'll just pull back out.

He even notices some form of relief, now that what he has long since foreseen actually appears to be happening:

a very direct and transparent payment platform, the diametric opposite to what the banks are offering. A new kind of financial institution like this has always been in the back of his mind, but he never made it a reality. He sees a well-functioning straightforward payment system as a first step away from the danger of the current oligopoly. If they can get it to work, the market will be open to new services, which will greatly benefit society as a whole.

Docters van Leeuwen has struggled for years with the way in which the banking model has developed. The oligopoly, the focus on short-term profits, the mixing of the business and retail bank in a single organization, the stripping of the internal mechanisms of control...

He finds that, because essentially nothing has changed, the problems we've been aware of since 2008 still persist. The risks remain great and measures such as increasing the financial buffers are applied so sparingly, that they barely help. It feels like plastering over the cracks instead of implementing the necessary structural improvements. A future crisis will be even worse.

Is this not what anthropologist Joris Luyendijk, after the two hundred interviews with London's City bankers, which he held for *The Guardian*, also found to be the case? It led him to the inevitable conclusion: 'This Can't Be True' – the Dutch title of his book *Swimming with Sharks*. The financial world is a 'virtual cluster of islands in the fog' with the potential of forcing the 'real world' over the precipice.

Besides being dangerous and outdated, the current situation is, according to Docters van Leeuwen, also bizarre: Give me your money, and I'll go off and do something with it. You get something in return, but I'm keeping the rest. It's strange that banks are still intermediaries in this. Not to mention the fact that consumers have nothing to say about it, not even now that many of the larger banks have been – either partially or fully – nationalized. This despite the fact that in the rest of society, he does see people acting of their own accord, like when it comes to the stock market. He increasingly hears of activities whereby an intermediary is no longer necessary, or as in banking services, even unwanted. But still, this anti-bank attitude? They need to let that go. It's all very well when you're looking to define your own identity, but it will spark opposition and impede success. It's precisely as Machiavelli writes in *Discorsi*:

> 'One of the most sensible things a man can do, is to refrain from threatening or insulting language, as neither of these two weaken the enemy: threats make him more watchful, and insults will feed his hatred.'

For Project Clear, Docters van Leeuwen's surprisingly fast commitment is a huge stamp of approval. The dream has suddenly become a lot more realistic. But however great of a step forward this is, they will soon find that there is still a long road ahead.

Coding is Your Life

Docters van Leeuwen coming on board has been a massive boost. Ali writes a Facebook status appeal to the universe: 'Bring on the future, 'cause I am all outta patience!'.

Attila, Peter and Long are spending every waking hour on the demo and the system architecture. All three of them have become skilled at Scala, and they're mainly focusing on the iPhone, the 'biggest and coolest platform around' in Attila's book. It's creative work. They program, try out, tweak and polish. What do you want the app to look like on the surface and how do you want it to be used in practice? The picture continues to change as they go through the infinite loop of 'imagine, create, test and perfect'.

The demo for Docters van Leeuwen is merely a prototype. It's a newly devised first impression of a seemingly simple, but actually complex service. The first and final versions of the app may look alike on the surface, but they'll be completely different in the way they function after months of expansion and adaptation.

To draw Ali's 'new dawn' closer, they need more coders and they need them soon. The issue has become more pressing since Pjotr, Duke's brother, decided to leave Project Clear. He has a two-hour daily commute each way, which, combined with the long working hours, is a perfect mix for battle fatigue. More often than not he sleeps in the freezing office, on a stretcher he brought from home. It's breaking him up and making him lose his temper, especially with Ali, who seems to have zero sympathy for his struggle. Duke is more understanding of his brother's situation, but doesn't get too involved. Their territories have been clearly defined and he doesn't want to overstep the mark.

Pjotr's departure lands a large chunk of the IT responsibilities on Ali's shoulders. Besides managing the other coders, he's now having to pitch in on the practical side.

TransIP can't afford to lose any more coders without compromising its quality, so Djoeri places an online vacancy straight away. The level of response is disappointing. To get the right people in, they need to up their game in terms of recruitment and selection, so Djoeri decides to place an HR ad instead.

Guido, a 27-year-old from the south of the Netherlands, responds. He has a good job at stock-market-sweetheart Booking.com, but he feels out of place. Over the years, the travel website has grown into a gigantic organization, making HR a completely separate and over-regulated department. Guido, in search of more freedom and creativity, browses the web for vacancies and stumbles upon Project Clear. His application is like manna from heaven.

As a Trans-IPer, Djoeri is well aware of Ali's demands when it comes to employees. They have to be young, on the ball, driven and show plenty of initiative. Smoking's out of the question: you feel the need to die? Do it in your own time. So Djoeri and Guido ask themselves: what would draw applicants like those to a place like this?

'Idealism, adventure,' Djoeri suggests. 'We shake things up, it's what we do. We're unconventional and that's exactly what appeals to them.' Guido concludes that the vacancy just wasn't sexy enough. They write a new one.

> **Software Developer at our international start-up in Amsterdam**
>
> This is a unique opportunity to be part of an international start-up based in Amsterdam. Fueled with ambition, we are bent on writing history.
>
> As our developer, you will have the chance to work with the absolute best. You have a real passion for programming. Coding is your life, inventing is your hobby. We are looking for a go-getter, teeming with energy, who learns quickly. You are curious by nature and have always been bored at school.
>
> You will join the team that develops our secure and scalable high-availability systems. The sky is the limit: if you have the skills, we will give you the freedom and responsibility to work on ambitious projects. This could be your chance to be part of a game-changing initiative, if you are up for it.

One of the first people to spot the vacancy is Sergey, a warm-blooded man with an icy gaze, from St. Petersburg. Despite having lived in the Netherlands for twenty years, he barely speaks a word of Dutch. When he does, by rare exception, utter a phrase or two, his words are weighted with strong rolling 'Rs', 'eys' and 'oys', like 'drroyverrs loyshensh'. His colleagues secretly suspect that he masters the language much more than he lets on, but they haven't managed to get more than a few words out of him.

He carries his past in his voice, but he's no talker. An unrequited love drove him to the West. Whether he ran the distance or cycled it remains a mystery, as he's passionate about both. Given half-decent weather, he rides his bicycle the full forty miles from The Hague to Amsterdam, and he tends to start work at 8 am, not leaving the office until well after 10 pm.

'Coding is your life, inventing is your hobby. You are curious by nature and have always been bored at school.'

The line also reaches Petros, a Greek. At this point, his future as he imagined it is as good as ruined. His ambition, however, is not. In Athens, he and two partners developed a search engine for fashion – an unlikely choice, judging by his casual appearance. The company was in full swing for three years and still continued to develop. However, when the time came that they needed a new injection of capital, it never arrived. Money dried up, and foreseeing an endless struggle, Petros pulled the plug. Disillusioned, he left his roots behind at the age of 33. While the crisis was hitting his own country with a vengeance, he boarded a plane to London in search of greener pastures.

Petros is stopping off at a friend's house in Amsterdam when he comes across Djoeri and Guido's vacancy. Without so much as a blink, he throws himself headlong into a new future with Project Clear. Like Sergey, he has a strong accent, turning 'google' into 'ghughol'. He turns every working Sunday into a feast with his mean cooking skills and fair share of tequila-related anecdotes to compensate for the lack of alcohol.

Resolutely and rigorously, Ali tightens his grip on the reins of the IT department. He decides to erase all of the programming they had. Hundreds of thousands of lines will need to be re-written. Why?

According to Ali, the fact that the coding process has

been so experimental and explorative has rendered the result useless as a basis to work from. For example, Attila and Peter have developed a code that allows you to make a payment by shaking your phone. It's tricky to use and, on reflection, won't be used in future. And if you're not using it, it shouldn't get in your way later on.

Code is sensitive. A story or a poem may survive a typo or a badly chosen word or sentence, and even a crappy paragraph doesn't necessarily ruin the whole thing. Programming language, however, is much more delicate. In the same way that one little copying error in DNA can lead to a defect or complete failure to function, a single mistake in the code can unravel your entire system. So if there are too many glitches, you're better off wiping the slate clean and starting over, line by line, than trying to find and correct each individual error.

The first quarter of 2013 is marked by a number of banking failures in the Netherlands. SNS bank is plagued by transaction delays, Rabobank's clients are locked out of online banking, even on their smartphones. ING's systems are difficult to reach for weeks on end, and to top it all off, payments by over half a million clients are suddenly debited twice.

Most of the issues are blamed on cyber-attacks. The banks rush to try and protect themselves by setting up firewalls all over the place. The Public Prosecutor orders a High Tech Crime Prevention Team to investigate the attacks. In the meantime, the National Cyber Security Center tries to disable the 'botnets' – large networks of servers, which are able to carry out coordinated attacks using malware. Even the Secret Service chips in where they can.

In most cases, they turn out to be dealing with so-called DDOS attacks: Distributed Denial of Service. These redirect all kinds of random internet traffic to one specific website, creating bottlenecks and making the website in question unreachable. They're not so much dangerous as they are annoying. The whole thing could be compared to a Facebook appeal for everyone to go and stand in line for a specific cash register. This leads to long queues at that specific register, making a quick payment impossible. But it says nothing about the safety of the money inside the cash register.

Wiebe Draijer, Chairman of the Social Economic Council and in the running for Chairman of the at Rabobank, calls the problems a 'wake-up call' for governments and banks. Hans Biesheuvel, Chairman of SME-Netherlands, comments that the malfunctions in payment traffic 'really have to stop'. 250 million euros circulate in retail every day. So a profit loss of 'just' a few percent has a massive impact.

According to experts, the malfunctions can't be blamed on 'third-party attacks' alone. They are also, even mainly, caused by the instability of the banks' own systems.

The banks, constantly growing and merging, have been piling system on top of system for years. This has made the systems complicated, outdated (like any IT system after a few years), vulnerable and hard to improve. The banks have no choice but to mend and make do, leaving their systems under-protected.

It makes sense: if you're going to build a house, you can't go changing the foundations and moving bearing walls around after you've finished it. The stability and expandability of the structure need to be included in the blueprint. It's the same for system architecture.

Some malfunctions are the result of simple clumsiness: the double-debiting turned out to be caused by a full hard drive...

Even TransIP turns out not to be immune to outside threats. They, too, take a severe DDOS beating. The company manages to fend off the initial attacks, but when the invisible opponent turns on their hosting servers, it takes down their own website for a while. Ali's bricking it.

To its credit, TransIP manages to keep its client side systems running despite the skillfully played game of cat-and-mouse. As importantly: they offer transparency early on, notifying their clients even before any of them run the risk of being inconvenienced, a decision that earns the company a huge amount of sympathy and trust.

Ali sees the entire nightmare as a baptism of fire, preparing him for what's ahead: 'This is how I want to do it: direct and honest contact with everyone who uses our app. From the day we go live.'

Inner Circle I: *The Powers that Be*

Project Clear is taking on the establishment. So it will need to be able to protect and defend itself from possible media attacks and orchestrated criticism planned by outsiders. Duke and Ali are aware of their need for a shield of powerful and influential friends, who share their ideals and are willing to serve as sounding boards now and again. Friends who may even be willing to lobby and vouch for them.

Over fifty people are gathered on the evening of April 16, 2013 for the first 'Inner Circle' meeting. They have all signed the non-disclosure agreement.

Ali does the introduction. Project Clear, he explains, has now been operational for four months and was established half a year ago. He introduces the teams — eleven people in total — and begins his presentation. A projector spouts newspaper headings from the last few weeks across a screen in bold capitals. Cyber-attacks on banks are an international phenomenon. Even Bank of America, Citibank and Chase have suffered. If such first-class institutes are vulnerable, where does that leave Dutch banks? And, more importantly, where will it leave Project Clear?

His media snapshots of targeted banks are met with uncomfortable recognition. 'This,' Ali points out, 'these flatlined systems, are just the sort of thing Project Clear wants to fix,' and he moves onto a slide that reads their profession of faith: Why does Project Clear exist? To fix market inefficiencies. To create transparency in the financial sector. To boost consumer welfare. To increase ease of payment. To focus on service instead of profit. To prevent malfunctions. For safe banking.

It's bank jargon, except for the final bullet point, just appearing onto the screen: To boldly go where no man has gone before – Star Trek. The room is filled with financials, wishing them a safe trip as they venture into new worlds.

'The application process for the banking license is due to start in a few weeks,' Ali continues. They're prepared. By the end of 2013, the system will be live, and the start-up will have taken just over a year. World domination is planned for the 1st of January 2018 — sooner is also fine. He reaps his applause as he proudly reports that Docters van Leeuwen will be heading the Supervisory Board.

Then, Peter takes over the pointer. What he is about to do on his iPhone will be displayed on the screen via a live feed. It's the first public demonstration of uncharted territory: purely mobile payment. 'Simple, intuitive, user-friendly and safe.'

Peter goes to his contacts, selects a name, enters an amount, and with a swipe of his finger the payment is sent. A second projected smartphone utters a pleasing ping to alert the owner of the received payment. Directly, without any intervention, the amount has been credited to the other smartphone. As a final showpiece, Peter shows the audience how easy it is to invite someone to pay the modern way via your contact list. A loud round of applause follows.

Duke, who watched the entire presentation standing up, feasts on the applause. But how worthy of acclaim is what they showed, really? The demo is a gadget, nothing more. After four official months, the entire IT infrastructure is still to be developed and a banking permit is nowhere to be seen. The financing is falling behind and every passing week costs money. The Inner Circle has just been promised that Project Clear will be going live in eight months. Is that prognosis not just as naive as the four weeks originally planned for the licensing process?

Ali takes back the floor: 'We still have a few challenges ahead. The security, a possible exponential growth of users, affecting scalability and system demands, and pretty much the entire IT infrastructure. Also, we still need to work the market and, oh yeah, get our hands on a banking license. The good news is: we have a name. From now on, we're called *Bright Bank*!'

Then follows an Oprah-moment: everyone gets their very own Casio F-91W. The Inner Circle members are officially unified with Bright Bank.

License of Goodwill

Bright:
1 shining with much light: *"bright sunshine."*
2 (of a colour) strong and bold: *"a bright red car."*
3 cheerful: *"a bright smile."*
4 clever: *"bright children."*

The name Bright Bank – an idea of Ali's – was a surprise, even to some of Project Clear's pioneers. Didn't they want to avoid being associated with traditional banks at all cost? Even rebel against them, from their outdated systems to their faulty culture?

But it turns out there is a reason behind the madness: 'Bright' and 'Clear' are close together in both meaning and association. The 'bank' add-on is to indicate that they want to be more than just a PSP, Payment Service Provider, reliant on existing banks. Bright young kids as they are, they want to tell a different story. Everything perfectly clear. Payments with just a smartphone or tablet. Inspiring, modern. One central service. Continuous dialogue with the customer. Risk free.

Internally, the name flops. Everyone continues to talk about Project Clear or 'the app'.

Jordi is a lawyer. With his fancy suit and his deliberate, posh-sounding language, he's the archetype of the career man who focuses on, or is at least associated with, money and success. His first day at Alex Asset Management Bank began, as it did for his fellow newbies, with the full two hours and thirteen minutes of *Wall Street*: the 1987 film about Bud Fox (Charlie Sheen), who wants to make it as a stock trader working with Gordon Gekko (Michael Douglas): 'The point is, ladies and gentlemen, that greed, for lack of a better word, is good. Greed is right, greed works. Greed clarifies, cuts through, and captures the essence of the evolutionary spirit.'

Jordi was in a room with the quick thinkers. They were nothing compared to the real sales guys, who were presented with *Glengarry Glen Ross*, from 1992: 'We're adding a little something to this month's sales contest. As you all know, first prize is a Cadillac El Dorado. Anyone wanna see second prize? Second prize is a set of steak knives. Third prize is you're fired. Get the picture?'

After a crash course, Jordi entered the firing line as a broker. He spent half a year on the phone with nervous sweat dripping down his forehead. After being promoted to a 'senior-operational-manager-kind-of-function', he switched to law firm De Brauw Blackstone, for the kind of unspoiled legal work that moved him a little closer to the edge of his seat. He provided counsel to organizations that were in trouble with the supervisors, AFM or DNB. The trouble was often over squabbles such as market abuse (with or without intent) or market manipulation, also known as rate manipulation.

The sudden death of his father made him question and reflect. *How much do I really enjoy my job? Does it give me enough energy? Or do I do it so that I can spend Friday nights bragging to my friends about how hard I worked and the importance of the cases I handled?* Just at that moment an email arrived from Duke — the timing couldn't have been any better:

> Hi Jordi, (...) we're looking for an enterprising lawyer for (international) licensing processes and general matters of corporate law such as IP, compliance and possibly M&A/ financing. Teaser: www.projectclear.nl. Interested?

Jordi is certainly interested. He gets the non-disclosure agreement shoved under his nose and Duke gives him the lowdown. All becomes clear when Ali's brought into the room. Jordi gets an offer and signs on the spot.

The rush may be absurd, but his arrival is much needed. Four months after the decision to go for a banking license, not a single step has been climbed on the application ladder, and the costs are mounting. The piece of paper from the DNB is the absolute prerequisite for providing banking services. Without a license, Project Clear can do no more than develop a funky little IT gadget and hook it up to some existing bank's system. That would mean dependency, as well as costs, undermining the entire business model. Besides, their app would have to stay within the technical boundaries of the banks, so it would end up no different from any other mobile banking system.

At home, Jordi deliriously recounts his meeting, without being allowed to actually say anything substantial. It results in gibberish. Within a week, he left De Brauw Blackstone with full knowledge that his new adventure will be over in a heartbeat if he doesn't deliver. But he reasons, he's 28 years old, no house, no kids. The kick and the experience far outweigh the risk.

On his first day at Project Clear, Ali shoves a MacBook Air into Jordi's hands: 'So you're responsible for the licensing process. Good luck.'

Jordi makes his way to the storage space, hidden in a poorly lit parking garage underneath the office tower, to find a table, and at the very least, three acceptably stable chairs. He drags them into the fickle lift, squeezes in, vigorously hits the '2' a few times and slowly rattles his way up three floors. Once arrived, he drags his loot to an empty room and installs himself between the door and the window. He opens the laptop. The MacBook works. He's been configuring it for a while when Duke enters his room. They agree on a timeline for the license application: about four weeks. Again, it's 'Good luck!' and Duke's off.

Jordi buys a version of Word online.

Ali walks by again and spots him in a typical waiting-for-the-download-to-finish position. 'Still haven't started yet?' he asks in an intrusive tone and disappears again.

Finally, a flashing cursor appears on the screen. Jordi takes a couple of deep breaths. *What does a sensible person do? Make a to-do list. What does one need for a banking license application?*

He pulls up the necessary legal information online.

Thanks to Jordi's arrival, Daan can fully focus on drawing up the business model. How does a bank account work in relation to the central bank? Which departments do existing banks have, and which of those are useful to Project Clear, aka Bright Bank? How do mobile payment methods work in the Netherlands and beyond? How will Project Clear/Bright Bank be different in this respect to others and how will that translate to paper?

Traditional banks make money from money. They attract it, lend it, invest it and make up complicated constructions to be able to keep as much of it as possible in the process. Making money from money is their core activity and at the same time, the main reason for the fundamental and ongoing failure of banks. It's the reason they're a liability to society. Because the more risks they take, the higher their potential profit.

The essence of every commercial company is, of course, to make a profit. But every company also knows that too many risks or wrong decisions lead to bankruptcy. Banks, however, occupy a special position. If they take too many risks or make mistakes, society pays the bill. This imbalance makes for a dangerously toxic cocktail.

Project Clear/Bright Bank wants to get rid of that principle by only making money from transactions and subscriptions. That way, profit maximization is only dependent on them creating a product that people actually want to use. This rules out loans or overdrafts, because that would mean taking unnecessary risks with someone else's money, which would be way too similar to the 'old style' of banking.

The catch-22 is this: the DNB as well as Dutch law name 'the attracting and lending of money' as a prerequisite for a banking license.

Jordi consults his network. His best friend's brother is a partner at law firm Simmons & Simmons, and he tells Jordi not to worry: if you attract money, you're obliged to do something with it, but what you do is up to you... Store it at DNB. That way you have a debt-claim over DNB. In other words, you lend the money to DNB and with that, meet the requirement. Voilà. Theoretically and legally, the solution seems solid. However, all the other lawyers he speaks to advise him to bypass the problem altogether; start out as a payment service provider and then, after a few years, become a bank. Duke, too, is past this option. He's had this discussion with Ali, and he lost.

The teams Duke and Ali discussed for nights on end are beginning to take shape. Before their recruiting offensive, there were two teams: 'IT' and 'Overhead'. Team Overhead covered everything that wasn't IT.

Team Overhead has now split up into HR, Finance and Legal. Team Marketing and Team Business Development are also starting to emerge. Team IT is a constant and expanding factor. Duke is responsible for Finance, Legal and Business; Ali's in charge of IT, HR and Marketing. Everyone has their set of tasks.

Duke is also head of license application. Docters van Leeuwen has a coaching function in this DNB process. He comments on the documents and offers advice on the plans. All IT-related content comes from the coders, who map out the processes with Ali.

They spend a lot of time trying to translate their ideas to Excel. Excel is the truth of the financial world. Daan finds a nice quote about it in *Life's a Pitch* by Stephen Bayley and Roger Mavity.

> 'Counting is what bankers do. They don't come from a country inhabited by human beings with human emotions. They come from a very different place called Spreadsheet

> Land where numbers are what matter. If you can measure it, analyze it, audit it, then in Spreadsheet Land that's good. But if you need an act of imagination rather than an act of arithmetic to grasp the idea, then that's bad. Show a banker an old idea and he will probably dismiss it on the grounds that it isn't new. But show him an idea that is new, and he will definitely dismiss it on the grounds that it is unproven. And unproven means, "I can't count it, I can't measure it."'

In order to prepare for their contact with DNB, Docters van Leeuwen suggests CLCS: Compliance & Legal Consultancy Services. In a rectangular canal-side house, sandwiched between two clock gables in the heart of Amsterdam, Duke and Jordi meet with a set of very charming and enterprising former AFM supervisors with an air of expertise; two women and a man. They claim to be able to advise on risk management, laws and regulations and management structure, as well as offer consultancy for license applications. No-one so much as blinks when Duke explains that they want to start a bank, not even when he adds: 'But a completely different bank from the existing kind. Ours is fully mobile and purely service-based.'

To Duke and Jordi's direct question: 'How do you do that?' they receive a very concrete answer: 'We have templates for that.'

During the following weeks, and with the help of CLCS, Jordi and Daan put together over one hundred densely printed pages full of information, covering every condition set down in law for the founding of a bank.

The cornerstone is the business plan: what will Project

Clear/Bright Bank be doing and how. Then there's the AO/IC handbook: the detailed structures of the Administrative Organization and the Internal Control, as briefly mentioned in the business plan. The third layer explains the handbook through outlining specific policies and internal regulation.

It's preparation, nothing more. At the moment, there is no contact with DNB yet and it's still unsure whether they'll even be allowed to apply.

However enterprising and specialized, the reassurance by CLCS that it's a mere question of filling out existing forms, turns out, after roughly six weeks and many thousands of euros in consultancy fees, to have been both premature and outdated.

Not only does Project Clear/Bright Bank want to be an entirely different kind of bank, the world has also changed significantly since the last license was issued. The CLCS templates were designed for classic banking, from the prehistoric days before the financial crisis. They don't have predefined fields for different kinds of earning models or fully mobile systems.

Having covered a lot of familiar ground with CLCS, Jordi and Daan are about to enter into uncharted territory without a road map. As kick-starter and driving force, CLCS has been very useful. However, it slowly transpires that they will need to invent a new wheel altogether, something the Project Clear/Bright Bank boys consider themselves to be good at. They're more free-spirited, or even: younger, smarter and better. They have a clear picture of what they want. Now they just need to get it.

That, however, turns out to be quite a challenge. Especially when Ali commits an almost fatal 'stupidity'. In an unfortunate moment, he jeopardizes everything they've fought for so far. Younger, smarter and better? Not him, not anymore. Ali is suddenly a blind painter, a deaf composer. He takes a fall that turns out to be a pivotal moment in his life, and very nearly the end of Project Clear/Bright Bank.

THE STRUGGLE

Headaches

A loud ringing cuts through the void in Ali's head, as if a bomb just went off next to him.

When he opens his eyes, he's surprised he's still alive. There she is, lying next to him on the pavement. Ali takes a few deep breaths, scrambles up and staggers towards her. He asks her if she's alright. 'I'm okay,' she says, but he can hardly hear her.

Ali stumbles back into the bar, asks for some ice and covers his eye with his hand. It's 2 am on a cool April's night in the city of Groningen. He tests his left eye, then his right. What day is it again? There's blood on his hands. He feels rough and asks for some water.

Thijs, designer at TransIP and a recent addition to Project Clear, suggests they go to a hospital. Ali dismisses the idea and gets a cab to direct them to their hotel. Despite feeling utterly horrible, he's still sharp enough to notice the driver swindling them out of a tenner.

In the hotel lobby, the security guard sends Ali and his bleeding head straight to a doctor, who performs the same tests as Ali already did. He covers one eye first, then the other, and diagnoses him with a mild concussion. At worst – or so he claims.

As he staggers back to the waiting car, Ali realizes he didn't even get a tetanus shot. Never before has he felt this miserable, nauseous and dizzy.

The next morning, having barely slept, Ali coughs up blood. The taste lingers in his mouth and throat for the rest of the day. He can't get a single thought straight. That night, after his brother Amir drove him to Amsterdam, he coughs up blood again.

He calls the out of hours doctor's service (it's Sunday), states his name, how he feels and what happened. They were outside. A friend, who just quit smoking, reached for her cigarettes. He wriggled the packet from her hands to tease her. A few minutes later, she grabbed them back, took a quick step backwards and tripped.

In his mind's eye, Ali could see her head slam into the stones. He stepped forward to break her fall, but she pulls Ali off-balance and down with her. The movement of her arm accelerated his fall. She landed softly, but he... in the middle of his rapid fall, Ali realized how entangled they were. That he wouldn't be able to catch himself because her arm was in front of his. That this would end badly.

He doesn't feel nor hear the crack of his head hitting the curb.

'Is your nose broken,' asks the operator. He explains that the blood isn't coming from his nose, but from his mouth. Twice, he mentions suspecting that this indicates something serious. 'Nothing to worry about,' says the operator. After all, the doctors are busy enough as it is.

After another terrible night, Ali calls his own doctor's office on Monday morning. His doctor has him come by immediately, gives him the tetanus shot and sends him straight to the hospital.

Ali has a skull fracture. A hole in his head the size of a ping pong ball, and his brain is numb. He can barely think.

A few days later, Ali sends a message to the world:

> 'Sincere thank you to everyone for the sympathy and heartwarming support. Careful, or I'll start thinking I'm not the stone-cold bastard people say I am. Given that I survived the first 48 hours, it appears as though I'll be sticking around for a bit longer. I'll keep everyone updated on the surgical plans! For now: sleep well.'

The email takes an immense amount of time and effort. The next day, he just about manages another:

> 'Good news today! As it turns out, the 2nd opinion doctor disagrees with the first one, whom he trained himself some years ago. He says that because the sinus is still intact I don't need the heavy surgery (had to be cut open from ear-to-ear). In fact: it will heal by itself, leaving an aesthetic mark that a plastic surgeon can fix. More good news: this has been verified by another Iranian and German surgeon too... Woohoo!'

Weeks later, the fall is still affecting Ali massively. He's drowsy and nauseous, his thoughts and movements are sluggish. He drags himself out of bed, answers three emails or phone calls and is exhausted within half an hour. He's continuously confused and distracted. Before the fall, his thoughts were agile and quick. Now they stumble and trip over each other like intoxicated kittens.

The constant struggle and fatigue drive him up the walls: 'I can't do anything anymore. Yeah, lie on the sofa with a pillow over my head. Brace myself, send a couple of emails and then crash again...'

Ali feels like someone else. When he looks in the mirror, he sees a face he doesn't recognize. His own thoughts and feelings are unfamiliar. His inhibitions have changed. He gets angry more easily, he's more impulsive. His speech is slurred, his sleep rhythm disrupted. He can only drive without music on. He even has trouble cooking. Thoughts don't come easily anymore. And once he finally has one, it immediately flits from his grasp. When he's having a conversation, he can't find the right words, they escape him like sand running through his fingers. In emails, he confuses words or puts them in the wrong order. He manages to read studies about brain damage, but he struggles to make sense of them. And then there's the pain... like a butcher remodeling his skull with a hammer drill. It's a nasty combination of a migraine-like headache and a hangover times a million.

At 9 am on Queen's day, the day of prince Willem-Alexander's coronation, the windows shake for eight long minutes at. The frigate Hr. Ms. Evertsen fires a 101 canon salute. Shortly after, ten F-16s come flying overhead in formation. Ali cringes. In the days and weeks that follow: floating helps, massaging helps, dry needling helps, Chinese medicinal tea helps and rest helps. He takes painkillers and avoids alcohol. Everything but his actual brain seems to leak from his cracked and then patched up skull. The timeline's gone, he's barely conscious of chronology or coherence.

Every now and then his introspection takes on hypochondriacal forms. He turns to self-examination and, at times, self-pity. 'In the middle of the night, I try to imagine how the hell I'm going to manage Project Clear and TransIP, try to figure out how I'm supposed to pull this shit off for the rest of my life...'

It's unclear for how long and to what extent Ali will be out of the running. His doctors don't think he'll ever completely recover. In any case, he has a fractured frontal sinus, just above his eyes, and he needs to prevent an overzealous jaw and skull specialist at the hospital from running a saw through his skull.

His brain is swollen, causing increased inter cranial pressure. His heart rate and blood pressure, as a result, are too low and fluctuate erratically. He should have been treated immediately in Groningen, and his doctors are baffled by the fact that he was sent home with a diagnosis of a 'possible mild concussion'. One of them speculates that Ali's name and appearance played a role in that process. This idea sows a seed of unfamiliar doubt in Ali. It makes him consider who he really is and how others perceive him. Is he 'Ali, the strong-willed, self-made man'? Or will he always be seen as the immigrant he never felt he was? Will he be truly accepted for who he is? Yes, a bit of an odd guy, but an alien?

What torments Ali the most: 'The greatest start-up ever has turned into the greatest fuck-up. We're barely halfway and I'm disabled on account of my own stupidity.'

Docters van Leeuwen, mainly concerned about Ali's wellbeing and secondly about the start-up, tells him to calm down and to give the recovery a chance. Not that Ali listens to him. How can he?

DNB has finally agreed to an introductory meeting.

The Managing Board at Project Clear/Bright Bank has effectively been reduced to one person: Duke. As Overall

Chief he manages to keep everything running, but the meeting with DNB deeply worries Ali. Will his new self have enough energy, will he have the wits to make the right impression, the right comments? Will he be analytical and fast enough?

He notices how his convictions are unchanged – but that too worries him. One of his life mottos is: there's an alternative to everything. Any goal you want to reach can be reached in different ways; round the back, from the front or straight through. And if that doesn't work, you go over the top or underneath. Giving up is failure, and failure is for the slackers, the lazy, the unimaginative and those who lack problem-solving skills, mostly due to one of the three aforementioned shortcomings.

But now? There is only one DNB. There is no alternative in the Netherlands, and they'll only get one chance. If he screws this up, they'll have to go to somewhere like the UK, and take the much more difficult route of trying to obtain a foreign banking license. That wouldn't have worried the old Ali. He had everything under control – himself included. The new, partly unknown one, is less poised. It takes all of Ali's efforts to control his emotions and his words.

And that's just the thing Docters van Leeuwen has been talking to Ali and Duke about from the beginning: that they should reconsider their choice of words. Docters van Leeuwen is still not a fan of their anti-bank attitude. If you want to beat the banks, the last thing you should do is advertise it. That will only create resistance and confuse the regulatory body. Your thoughts are your own business; keep them to yourself. He advises them to focus on the payment platform, which no one can object to, not even DNB.

The black-and-white attitude towards conventional banks is instrumental to the team in the office. Take the negative aspects of the existing parties and fight them with your own positive aspects. To change the things that bother you, you have to highlight them. It clarifies your approach. It's not about rebelling for the sake of it. It's about focusing all of the energy, intellect, time and means at the embodiment of contrast.

So: get rid of the tainted inheritance of the failing financial institutions. Away with their structures, their DNA, their profiteering policies, bonus systems, Libor rate manipulations, cluster bomb investments...

The idea of 'us vs. them' makes them feel like they can take on the world, from scratch. Free of responsibility for the financial, economic and moral crises, they can set up an organization and make it work the way they want it to, without limitations. It shapes them into a team, as Jordi calls it, 'all fighting under the same flag'. That's how you fight the established order. That's how a revolution begins. Provided, in this case, that it sticks nicely to the unwritten rules.

After a brief struggle, Duke and Ali agree to moderate their tone, but only outwardly. They formulate their feelings and thoughts differently, more diplomatically, with less blatant negativity – but the essence of their story and their criticism of banks remain the same. The best way to express their criticism is through proving that things can be done differently, done better. And so it becomes even more important that Project Clear/Bright Bank succeeds.

Can Ali keep up this moderate tone when he goes to DNB? Or will he fall victim to his new self: uncontrolled, plagued by headaches, nausea and exhaustion? Can he still reason with a sense of emotion and passion without losing it? Or will he pontificate that banks are a perversion of society that feed off people like parasites, existing at our expense and giving us nothing in return. Many at DNB are, were or will be bankers, and that worries Ali. By allowing his own beliefs to overcloud his mind, he risks making statements that will ruin any possibility of a decent relationship with DNB. So, he ponders, can I still afford to be myself?

First Contact

The Central Bank of the Netherlands or 'De Nederlandsche Bank' (DNB) is located in Central Amsterdam and occupies an entire block of buildings. Two office towers sit firmly rooted in a square, three-story base. One of the towers is rectangular with red tiles in horizontal lines. The other, built later, is round and reflects the surrounding sky. Because gold bars used to be kept here, the building is a complex fortress featuring half a moat, fencing and obstacle blocks disguised as a rock garden.

Duke and Ali stand facing the large silver rotating doors, galvanized with fiberglass. Trapped in the glass, they see their own reflections and those of a row of canal-side houses. Over their heads, the office floors lean their heavy weight on concrete pillars.

They show their IDs in the lobby. There are cameras, heavily armed military police wearing bulletproof vests and carrying automatic rifles, and a smiling receptionist. They're allowed in. They're told to follow — which they obediently do, they introduce themselves once more, and then they sit. Waiting. Two DNB employees join them a bit later, sitting across the table. They're from the accessions department. An excerpt of the brand new business plan is laid out in front of them. It's by this plan that the two members of the Bright Bank Managing Board mean to show DNB how they will be doing things differently. Completely differently. As agreed, Duke does the talking.

They want to know what their chances are and how long

the procedure is likely to take. The DNB employees want to talk about the CEO/majority shareholder relationship. This concerns Ali's position, as he is both. Just like Dirk Scheringa at DSB (a bank that went bust). With one difference: Dirk Scheringa took money out of the bank to fund his private hobbies, whereas Ali puts private funds into the business. But just because it hasn't happened yet doesn't mean it couldn't, and DNB would rather be safe than sorry.

Duke explains the business plan, the DNBers ask questions to better understand the picture. Then they roughly map out the application procedure.

Ali's never been this nervous in his life. It's hard to concentrate and he's tired and nauseous within the first few minutes of the conversation. He keeps quiet, by which he unknowingly removes the reason for his nerves: this way, at least, his emotions can't get the better of him.

They're out the door in just over half an hour. With mutual consent, they decide to start out with a conceptual application, before submitting the final license application: after all, none of the four conversation partners had even made it through puberty the last time anyone completed the entire application process.

Duke returns to the office to cover the day-to-day management. Ali rushes home. He's pale, his eyes are rigid, but he's relieved. His worries have proven unfounded, just like his idea of DNB. He was expecting 'bankers', conservative minds, and found interest and willingness with a hint of caution. Back at his apartment, he falls asleep on the sofa for hours. Wrecked.

In order not to stray too far from their original schedule,

Duke and Ali want to file the conceptual application within six weeks. A month-and-a-half to build a bank: management structure, risk analyses, terms and conditions, the whole nine yards. A ton of paperwork at least thirty times the size of their business plan, which took them six months to produce.

DNB sends over a checklist with over a hundred questions. Each requires multiple documents, ranging from a certified copy of the statutes, a list of activities, screenings and guarantees with regard to the management and commissioners (such as a suitability matrix for the Managing and Supervisory Board), to a description of the control structure and a full overview of the internal control. Additional requirements include a declaration of private funds, solvency and liquidity and a pile of declarations of no objection.

Each section comes with sub-sections. For the 'description of the organization of management with regard to controlled and incorruptible corporate practice', for example, the following attachments apply:

	Handbook AO/IC
Annex 1	Regulation Notification of Incidents
Annex 2	Regulation Use and Review of Communication Tools
Annex 3	Remuneration Policy
Annex 4	Complaints Procedure
Annex 5	Conflicts of Interest Policy
Annex 6	Client and Transaction Monitoring Policy
Annex 7	Regulation Screening and Integrity-sensitive Positions

Annex 8	Regulation Private Investment Transactions
Annex 9	Procedure Recruitment of Members of the Managing and Supervisory Board
Annex 10	Product Approval Process
Annex 11	ICAAP Manual
	Risk Matrix
Annex 12	ILAAP Manual
Annex 13	Data Processing Policy
Annex 14	Regulation Registration of Conversations
Annex 15	Business Continuity Plan
Annex 16	Workflows
Annex 17	Information Security Policy
	IT Risk Matrix
	Information Security Plan
	Information Security Reporting Overview
Annex 18	Incident Manual
Annex 19	ALM Policy
Annex 20	Whistleblowing Procedure
	Assignment Letter KPMG
	Policy Handling of Employee Data
	Anti-Bribery and Corruption Policy

These are only some of the attachments of a sub-section. The total amount of forms to be submitted is a multitude.

The time frame Duke and Ali have decided on is partly due to finances. Each passing day equals money spent and opportunity lost. Bright Bank is receiving a money transfusion from TransIP. There's plenty where that came from, but that can't be an excuse not to knuckle down. And as equally important, every wasted day increases the risk of a similar initiative in the market. ING, Rabo, ABN Amro,

Apple, PayPal, Google: they're all working on the further development of their own mobile systems. It's only a matter of time before those new systems appear on the market. As long as these develop along the same lines with the existing technology, such as NFC (Near Field Communication) chips, there's no need to panic. But one might expect someone up in Silicon Valley to be working on something similar, right?

Their meeting with DNB is soon followed by an introductory meeting with the AFM, Netherlands Authority for the Financial Markets. Bart, advisor at Deloitte and the guy who got them in touch with Docters van Leeuwen, facilitates the meeting and joins them. The business plan is sent in advance.

Within fifteen minutes, they're in the middle of an energetic discussion on the content. For once, the focus is not on the procedures or proportions, but on the needs of the consumer. At the end of the meeting, the AFM points out that DNB 'will be taking the lead', while consulting with the AFM. It's one of the changes following the DSB affair.

Jordi is in the lead for the application with Daan as his trusty sidekick. They soon realize that DNB's requirements differ considerably from what the law stipulates. The law requires a 'description' of an incorruptible and controlled corporate practice, while DNB needs everything to be worked out in detail already – rendering the CLCS templates useless.

DNB also claims that the 'realness' of a bank, a pre-requisition of the banking license, is based on the attraction of claimable funds and the subsequent lending of such funds for profit: the basic formula of a money factory. Bright Bank wants to diffuse this potential bomb from under its foundations by storing the attracted funds with DNB. This however, says the supervisor, is not enough to be considered a bank.

The brainteaser is back.

In order to charge independent tariffs to private and corporate clients, having a banking license, and thus officially being a bank, is essential. Only then can they develop their subscription model. But a main condition is that they make money on the back of other people's money – and they simply don't want to do that. So, now what?

Daan suggests that Bright Bank could, like a normal bank, lend money to small and medium enterprises (SMEs). This is the industry that will profit most from what they will put on the market, as they will no longer need expensive, physical payment systems. They could probably make solid agreements with an SME, and they could lend against the lowest possible rate.

But they won't. Absolutely not, as Duke reiterates to Daan and Jordi. Lending money comes with risks, which means having to attract capital in order to cover those risks. Then they're back to being just another bank, which they don't want to be: messing around with other people's money.

Jordi spots an alternative solution. Bonds: the safest kind, government bonds from stable countries such as the Netherlands and Germany. Investing in government bonds, in his eyes, is like extending credit. The risk is minimal and therefore acceptable. Any profits made on the government bonds – the yield at that time is zero percent – will in some way be returned to the clients. That way, Bright Bank acts free of risk and meets the DNB criteria. Right?

The weather takes it's own spin; whereas at the end of June there was still frost on the ground in some places, July 2013 arrives with a full on heat wave.

Dominik, a 25-year-old left-handed dutchified German, spots two LinkedIn vacancies on his PC in the southern city of Maastricht: asset manager at an established firm and something vague at a start-up. The latter strikes him as 'cool', as it connects his two main interests: IT and law. He calls both parties, hears Guido's southern accent and decides he will feel more at home in the latter's company, which in turn is looking for someone like him, as Jordi is in dire need of legal backup.

On a particularly hot day, Dominik travels to Amsterdam. At the office, the electric heaters have been stored away and a fridge is buzzing contently in a corner. Ali is amused at Dominik's vague likeness to the painter Van Gogh and calls him Vincent from the first moment he sees him. Guido subjects Dominik to an array of IQ and personality tests and, of course, a non-disclosure agreement. Dominik subsequently has a brief conversation with Duke and Jordi and, on that same Sunday, he relocates from Maastricht to The Hague, where he moves into a somewhat surprised friend's apartment.

'It's not a consideration, it's a conviction,' he explains to the latter. 'It's about the idea. What idea? I can't tell you...'

Dominik gets to write up the Administrative Organization. Daan and another rookie, Geert-Jan, throw themselves at the ever-expanding business plan. Geert-Jan, 26, studied at the Technical University of Delft and has a background in chemistry, innovation management and IT. For the last two of these disciplines he's plunged straight in the deep end, and in a very short time grows out to be a highly valued coder. Veteran Petros is added to the team for the descriptions of the operation and organization of the IT systems. Which safety procedures do you have in place? How do you validate a new client? A purely mobile bank has never been developed before, every task is revolutionary and an unknown path by itself.

Jordi, Dominik, Daan, Geert-Jan and Petros say their goodbyes to the outside world: for the foreseeable future, it'll be just the five of them, day and night.

'You're facing six incredible weeks,' Ali summarizes. 'We're all up for a challenge, but this will be crazy even by our standards.'

They take a group photo for Petros' friend, in which they hold up Petros himself and a note. The note is in Greek: 'Petros has been taken hostage. He will not be returning home until further notice.'

Wanted: Respectable CFRO

Besides producing an unbelievably tall stack of paper, Bright Bank needs to attract a number of new employees, fast. They need a lawyer with expert knowledge of the Financial Supervision Act to manage the license application. They are also pressed for a suitable CFRO — Chief Financial and Risk Officer – to complete the Managing Board. Without a CFRO, any conceptual license application is pointless.

The search for a lawyer has been ongoing since March 2013. Driven by the idea that long reputations strengthen the short one of a start-up, the focus has been on approaching only large firms.

The first conversation Duke and Ali had was with a partner at a renowned law firm, in early spring. To get him out of his comfort zone, they planned the meeting at a backpackers hostel. Then they opened the conversation with: 'What experience do you have and who do you know at DNB?' The smoothly suited and booted business partner was more of a bookish lawyer than a practical guy. He had expected them to be both overjoyed and honored to be able to meet him. This was not the case. The partner became more and more distressed and irritable by the minute. And so Duke and Ali decided to call it a day.

The problem has since become urgent. Jordi decides to widen the search for renowned lawyers. He calls an old colleague at De Brauw, who shares a few golden contacts with him, people whose books Jordi studied during his student days. People he quotes to back up his opinions. Nervously, he makes his first round of calls, detecting an unfamiliar incoherence in his own voice.

A number of named and famed firms seem interested. After all, it's a very prestigious project to be associated with.

Each is met with the same approach. First, Jordi talks to them 'lawyer-to-lawyer'. For a 'brief' forty-five minutes, he goes through a technical exploration of the requirements for a banking license application. At this point Ali refuses to attend because to him it's 'a waste of time'. Then Duke joins the party. He's a little less friendly, acting as bad cop to test people out. Then, finally, Ali makes his entrance. He's direct and gets straight to business, asking the difficult questions without detours or introductions.

Jordi hates that part. Ali's street fighter mentality makes his cheeks flush. But he knows it's tactics. Ali is gunning for gut reactions. Some respond calmly to the stress of his directness and map everything out clearly, others lose it. Using this method, it takes Ali just five minutes to see what they've got. If the reaction makes sense he smiles broadly, allows the atmosphere to change, then brings up payment. After all: 'We're a start-up and we can only spend our money once.'

But they never manage to get to the price negotiations. There turns out to be a widespread lack of practical experience in the legal handling of a license application.

Jordi enjoys the conversations academically, but acknowledges the fact that they involve an awful lot of lecturing. Ali thinks they're 'wasted breath and hot air'.

As the number of conversations progresses, his impatience turns into aversion. They all say the same thing:

we'll never get a banking permit, but we'll charge you an arm and a leg for trying. It's a way of covering their own asses. If they manage it, they've accomplished the impossible. If they don't, they already warned them in advance, didn't they?

Then, during the eighth interview, there's a click. At least with one person from the firm in question. She responds more than adequately to the mild provocations and shows more relevant knowledge than those before her. Duke and Ali have nearly lost faith, but Jordi emphasizes the authority she and her firm enjoy. Besides, he looks up to the scholarly lady.

He sends a letter of engagement and waits for an answer, in vain. After a week, he calls. No result. After another week, he goes by the office. Three weeks pass without a response. The lawyer in question is busy working on another case.

Duke and Ali have lost interest in the woman. A deal is a deal, you stick to it. No matter what. Jordi weighs up the overall picture: they're a start-up in an ad hoc office building. The plug on the project can be pulled at any given moment. Commercially it's unattractive. Other clients, like large banks, have deeper pockets and more pressing problems than Bright Bank.

Jordi gets to decide. He lets the firm know they'll not be working together. Only then does the *grand dame* whose books he knows inside out show her face. She wholly disagrees with the split and doesn't understand where it's coming from.

Bright Bank is back to square one and Jordi can feel the eyes burning into the back of his head. He is forced to turn to smaller firms, the niche players. Another process of elimination. Most want to send an invoice before they've even read the business plan and are rejected immediately. Down to even smaller firms, Jordi phones up Finnius Lawyers, 'specialized in financial law since 2010', where he is put through to Casper, a lawyer who turns out to have worked at DNB for thirty years.

Against all expectations, fifty-something-year-old Casper sails through the meeting with Ali. He stays on point, knows his stuff and remains calm. It doesn't just give Ali confidence in Casper himself, but in DNB as a whole. If someone like Casper managed to stay there for three decades, there may be more people there who can roll with the punches.

Meanwhile, Duke is on the hunt for the CFRO. The first stack of responses are from people who wouldn't even consider trading their careers for a lower-paid job without guarantees.

Duke is well aware that anyone who's anyone in the financial world is used to the reward structure that comes with it, and that such systems create certain dependencies and loyalties. To Ali, it's like talking to another species.

SCENE 01

Ad hoc office space. Empty table with chairs. Ali at short end of table, Duke at long end, candidate facing Duke. Ali and Duke shirt and jeans, candidate suit and tie. Candidate is in a relaxed position, arms resting on table. Long shot, then gradual close up on each.

DUKE

(slightly slumped)

So. We're looking for a CFRO who fits in with our culture. Who gets what we're trying to do.

ALI

(sits upright, restless)

Do realize that we're a start-up and actually want to become a new type of bank. We don't believe in bonuses and we find many of the current wages excessive.

CANDIDATE

(nods understandingly)

Camera briefly zooms in on his nearly empty cup of coffee.

CANDIDATE

450 thousand isn't that much, is it?

Silence. Close-up Ali.

ALI

(looks unfazed) VOICE OVER

Christ, he's serious! An average income is 30K per year. What's this idiot thinking? That he's worth 15 times as much as the next guy?

(gets up)

Thank you.

(exits room, leaves door open)

SCENE 02

Same office building and setup. Same camera technique.

ALI

(impatiently)

So. We're a service organization. That's what our earning model is based on. We don't just act differently, we are different. What's your take on that?

CANDIDATE

(nods uncertainly)

I don't understand. So how do you intend to lock in your clients? How do you lure them in?

ALI

(slightly irritated)

We don't think of it that way. We don't want

to 'lock' and 'lure'. We want to create a good

product that people actually want to use.

CANDIDATE

(nods and looks as though he understands)

No, of course not. But you have to reel
them in with something, right?

Silence.Close-up Ali.

ALI

(gets up)

Yeah, of course we do. NOT!

(exits room, leaves door open)

Five hundred and fifty CVs and personally or electronically rejected candidates plus a considerable number of informal networking conversations and meetings result in a meager list of three candidates who are willing and experienced. All three have an active career in the financial world.

Candidate One turns out to be surprisingly decent, sporty, intelligent, honest and amicable. In no way does he fit the stereotype of the arrogant banker. He is told that they would be very happy to have him on board as a financial director. Sadly, he comes with one large and insurmountable drawback: he is still fully occupied with a job at RBS, formally known as the Royal Bank of Scotland, rendering him unavailable in the short term.

Candidate Two is a smart, left-handed guy from the northern province of Friesland. Ali has a weakness for left-handedness. Ali attributes a unique worldview to the left-handed, albeit born of necessity: the world is a right-hand orientated place, after all. He praises their stubbornness, despite considering it to be draining and often misplaced. This candidate is also unavailable within Duke and Ali's time frame: immediately.

Candidate Three has just left his role as CFRO at a large financial institution. He's excited and sounds energized from his holiday address in Barcelona. Duke and Ali book the first available flight out to the Catalonian capital.

The trip is trying. Ali has ignored advice from his doctors as well as Docters van Leeuwen to rest. He slows down only when his exhaustion leaves him no choice. Sporadically floating and dry needling isn't making much difference: his head still feels like a taut drum, painfully amplifying every sound.

Schiphol Airport is mayhem; a cacophony of rattling cases, buzzing strip lights, screaming children and blaring metal detectors. The flight is even worse. Sandwiched in between other passengers, Ali can't escape the sounds and images around him. He spends the entire flight with Air Europa (or, as he calls it, the worst airline ever) with his fists clenched to his forehead, trying to block out the torture. When they arrive at El Prat de Llobregat Aeropuerto de Barcelona, the sound surges into his brain so violently that he nearly throws up.

The interview with candidate number 3 is an oasis of calm in comparison. The man mentions having managed to get a banking license once already, placing him miles ahead of the others. The fact that this was years ago, and by no means a greenfield venture, is irrelevant. When Duke tries to determine whether this former CFRO still has his edge, Ali (whose own edge has become a fraction of what it once was) dismisses his worries as defeatist.

The trip from hell pays off. With their new CFRO in the bag, they get on the first flight back to Amsterdam. Ali, once more, with his fists clenched to his forehead.

Less than a week later, Ali steps into Attila's office for an update on the coding for the app, which has been bugging him for a while. The first problem is wrapping his head around the code. Then, there's the actual content: the further he gets into the code, the more worried he becomes.

The code is written in Scala, marketed as 'compact and versatile, extremely suitable for complex tasks'. Ali's not into complexity. Intellect was created to simplify the complicated, not the other way around. Since his fall, he's had trouble getting his own mind in order, let alone trying to follow someone else's train of thought. The code is like a mirror of the chaos inside his mind. As though Attila somehow captured the damaged processes of Ali's brain and converted them into some kind of artificial intelligence.

Later that evening, Attila gets a text message: 'If you could start the whole thing again, write your own code, would you go with Scala?'

Naively, Attila responds: 'No, PHP'.

Despite the course in London and the months of working with Scala since, he's still much faster with PHP.

To him, the program's versatility makes it confusing and contradictory. The code is difficult to read in the long run, especially on big projects. Besides, PHP itself functions faster than Scala.

At 07:45 the following morning, Attila and the other coders receive an email: 'Now that we've decided to switch from Scala to PHP, there's a bit of a to-do list'.

Without consultation, Ali has thrown out another mountain of coding. All of the painstaking progress they've made on the app is reduced to scrap. As is the atmosphere in the office.

You Name It!

Ali's two-bedroom apartment by the waterfront of the IJ consists of a few basic bits of furniture on painted floorboards. The ceiling, with a couple of lonely light bulbs, is as bare as the floor. The walls, too, are empty, except for a large painting of a mysterious dark horseman in the living room. Photographs of friends or family are nowhere to be found.

Each piece of furniture — six dining chairs and a multi-seater sofa — serves as a work station for a man fused to his MacBook. Ali only uses his iPad to set up the playlist for his two enormous Linn speakers — or at least he did, before his fall, after that he couldn't cope with loud sounds anymore. His iPhone is always on his person, day and night.

Because of Ali's disturbed biorhythm, his already short nights are often spent awake. More than five or six hours' sleep is a rarity, though he spends a lot of time on the sofa since his fall. His bedroom is closer to the front door than the living room, shortening his bed-office commute. It's a small space with a large bed and heavy curtains. No photos here either, just a few piles of books on the floor. *Phases* and *Discorsi* have already made their way to the bottom of the 'finished' pile.

For the first time in weeks, he falls into a shallow slumber at half past midnight. An hour-and-a-half later, he finds he's been staring at the ceiling, his mind drowsy, but with his eyes wide open.

Slowly it dawns on him that he was woken up by a fleeting thought, like a tiny electric shock: image is more important than sound. Suddenly wide awake, Ali turns onto his left side and grabs his iPhone. The TransIP app shows that his brainwave is still available: bunq.

Bright Bank... a good example of how the (sub)conscious mind works: a spontaneous whim, a eureka moment, followed by a list of arguments thought up by the intellect to support it. Duke and Ali were so content with their idea that they concluded an Inner Circle meeting with it. But the name quickly lost its shine.

The 'bank' part was always dubious, but excluding it left too little to work with. 'Bright' has a good ring to it and seems clear, but it's hardly original. It felt too deliberate, too smooth, too obvious. The English atheist's society is called Bright. So is a Dutch gadget magazine and a series of cleaning products. 'Bright' as a term is impossible to protect.

More and more rational arguments appeared against the name — which the office insiders weren't using anyway.

And bunq? Image instead of sound. Messages no longer travel by word of mouth, but through images. Alliterations or Coca-Cola sounds are outdated. It's internet, not radio. Not a word, but an image. A name that functions as an image, a logo...

Thijs is a designer in his early thirties and, like Djoeri and Ali, he's officially employed by TransIP and travels back and forth between Leiden and Amsterdam. Ali shares his idea with him and the name: bunq. Thijs toys with the idea of a point symmetrical logo, which can be spun on its axis without changing. Identical from both sides of a smartphone or tablet — your side and that of the transaction partner. Mostly, he wants to avoid any separation of name and logo. His example is Nike, the name plus the symbol. That particular combination of name and logo was later separated.

Thijs decides to merge the concepts: he combines name and logo by making the letters visual, like graffiti or calligraphy. By not capitalizing the 'b', he gets his visual effect. He entangles the 'u' and the 'n' to symbolize two joining hands.

Ali is pleased as well with the fact that their logo doesn't meet some invisible list of expectations. After a few days, Thijs returns to his work of art. He knows that almost all good logos were created in a short space of time, and adjusted over a long period of time, or even continuously. To him, a logo never needs to be set in stone. Name or recognition won't disappear because of a few small changes. As long as there's no building bearing the name for all to see, you can continue to tweak and improve it.

Amir, Ali's brother, is a cognitive psychologist. Being an expert in cognitive processes, he subjects the logo to some non-scientific tests into legibility and reading time. Each time, he shows a few variants of the logo to a couple of people. He has his participants think aloud, in order to gain insight into their thought process. The only letter not causing any problems is the 'b'. The 'u' and the 'n' kept being seen as a single letter, causing some of the test subjects to read 'bing' or 'bang'. After each test, Amir reports back to Thijs, who then adapts the letters slightly, until eventually everyone says 'bunq'.

'So bunq you say? But what does the name mean?'

'Nothing! It's an expression of symmetry. We can find examples of symmetrical beauty everywhere in nature. Yet there's a deeper meaning as to why we find it beautiful: in a world as imperfect as ours, it's really hard to create two perfect 'mirror images'. External influences like temperature, bacteria, viruses and genetic mutations interfere with the process. That's why we're hardwired to like symmetry: it's a derivative of better adaptation to certain circumstances. It's why we like Scarlett Johansson. And other round things.'

The legible logo is created right on time.

After six exhausting weeks, Jordi and his crew, with the help of Duke and Ali, have managed to churn out a business concept that weighs over four kilograms after it's been printed. Docters van Leeuwen has read it and lawyer Casper has performed a legal sweep of the document.

The Managing Board is complete and even the Supervisory Board has been assembled. The search for two suitable commissioners turned out to be a lot less complex and time consuming than finding a lawyer and a CFRO.

Jan Docter, former CFO for Booking.com, is a contact of Peter's through his son. Something that incidentally came up in conversation over lunch. Jan Docter met with Duke and Ali, and when he heard of Docters van Leeuwen's involvement, he was instantly on board. They worked together on an assignment at the Ministry of Finance and he admires Docters van Leeuwen's intellect.

Emiel Roozen, financial director at Delta Lloyd, is a friend of Duke's. He too is enthusiastic, although he does need permission from Delta Lloyd for a possible commissionership.

Using find-and-replace, 'Clear' and 'Bright Bank' are changed into 'bunq'. The completed documents are altered just in time to be emailed off to DNB. Duke heads over to their office to deliver the information in person, too.

In ten months' time, what Duke calls 'an incredibly decent plan', foreseen by Docters van Leeuwen fifteen years ago, has been transformed into what Ali describes as 'FUCKING AWESOME'. He compliments everyone at the office at the top of his voice. 'What a team, what a drive, what an energy!'

Now the wait begins for DNB's response. Only that can prove how awesome the work has really been. If the response is negative, bunq will remain a fantasy for the time being...

Inner Circle II: *The Suicide Club*

The Royal Flying Corps, as the British Royal Air Force was called during World War I, was known as 'The Suicide Club'. In little biplanes made of wood, canvas and steel-wire, its young members circled over the front lines. There were no experienced pilots, nor was there a chance to become one. With fifteen hours of practice and an average lifespan of eleven days, there just wasn't time.

At the office, although the life expectancy of a newcomer is longer, the body count is high: not many make it through the thirty-day trial period.

The arrival of staff member number forty is celebrated, but twenty of those before him have already left. The bar is high. 'Be a yardstick for quality. Some people aren't used to an environment where excellence is the standard. We are', says the handbook.

At the start of 2013, Ali and Djoeri put a few things on paper to sum up the nature and strengths of the new company. The positive experiences from TransIP formed a checklist for the culture and structure they wanted; the bad experiences were noted down as pitfalls to avoid. Their notes grew into a handbook. Ali's influence on it is considerable. The passage on the anti-smoking policy is straight from his pen:

> 'We hate smoking. If you have to do it though, consider it a waste of your time and we ask you not to bother anyone else with it. If you want to quit smoking, we are supportive

and will do everything we can to get you through it. Since we hired you, we'd like to have you around. Not die of lung cancer or embolism.'

Their ambition to be a 'young, innovative, informal and service-orientated IT organization boasting an open culture, creativity and pragmatism' is broadly covered in the handbook.

OPEN CULTURE
We are proud of our open culture at bunq. An open culture benefits a young, audacious and fast-growing company such as ours. Also, good fellowship and creativity flourish in a non-restrained environment. Corporate hierarchy and formal ways hold back boldness, originality, ingenuity and personal development. We realize that an open culture such as bunq's is not to be taken for granted, especially not in the financial world. In order to maintain this open culture, we expect everyone at bunq to take care of company property and respect his or her colleagues. This way, rules and other red tape can be avoided. Make decisions honestly, honorably and consciously.

BE CREATIVE
Talented people create new ideas, fresh visions and discover new ways. Talent implies creativity and originality. So be creative! Treading on known paths will only lead to known results. We are innovative, so tread on new paths. These paths however do have to lead towards concrete results. Is it enough to be talented and creative? No, you also have to show results. Is it enough to be talented, creative and to

deliver concrete results? Hardly. Talent is the comparative of ingenuity. We want you to be a genius.

BE PRAGMATIC

Be pragmatic. You can discuss at length how something works or should work, only when it works you deliver the proof. We do not want 'religious' wars in the office nor see colleagues get trapped in right/wrong discussions. Therefore, you should not do things just because you have always done these things in a certain way, nor because you think that it will work. It has to work; otherwise it needs to be discarded. This means no theoretical discussions and endless intellectual exercises. Concepts remain theories until physically realized. Build and/or do it, and prove that it works.

Only one percent of applicants make it through the pre-selection and the following IQ and personality tests in the first place. Half of those actually manage to stay standing. The other half fail to prove themselves in practice.

Sometimes their work-pace is too low. Other times someone's specialism turns out to be mainly theoretical. Mostly it's a combination of not fitting into the culture and not learning fast enough.

Three 'high potentials' depart for the same — initially surprising — reason. They can't get used to working with other, similar high performers. At bunq, they're not the best of the best anymore, so the quality of their work no longer stands out. Guido watches their egos, dedication and confidence fade. They wither and disappear.

Sometimes there's an air of relief when a weak link

drops out, at other times, it's a true loss. When Peter, involved as a coder from day one, announces his departure to go back to New York, the news hits like a bomb. Everyone loves him and he's been crucial to the pioneering phase. But he's homesick.

At the second Inner Circle meeting, Ali announces that they've finally found a CFRO. 'Initially we reviewed three hundred profiles for this position. Later we added another two-hundred-and-fifty, followed by fifty interviews. From those fifty, only one suitable and available candidate remained!'

Although they're not all physically present, he also introduces the members of the Supervisory Board on a screen one by one. CVs and all.

Duke and Ali finally feel as if their 'strong team' is complete at every level – at least to cover the formal structures. But they also know that for the foreseeable future they will remain The Suicide Club; the formation will have to change along with the changes in the different phases they will find themselves in – each with its own challenges and its own brand of people.

Thijs is given the honor of presenting the bunq name and logo. As usual, the final showpiece comes from Ali.

Meanwhile a school has recently moved to the Arlandaweg, and their little sanctuary is suddenly very crowded. bunq's youthful appearance is now provoking a different kind of response. Guido and another bunqer ignore a red light as they cross the road. 'Can you please refrain from doing so again?,' a teacher reprimanded them, proceeding to ask the 'boys' which class they were headed to.

'It's time for us to grow up,' Ali promises. 'We're moving to a real office, four hundred meters down the road!'

Get Lucky

We've come too far
To give up who we are
So let's raise the bar
And our cups to the stars
We're up all night to get lucky
– *'Get Lucky'*, Daft Punk –

It's been five weeks after the conceptual application and there's still no reaction from DNB. In the last week the bunq team has grown impatient and restless. Not that they're short of things to do. With Petros back on board, the writing and improving of the code continues at a high pace. As part of his return initiation, Petros is fitted with a ball gag to keep him quiet. The toy from the S&M scene has the words 'typy typy' stuck onto it: more typing, less chatting.

Team Legal is already looking beyond the granting of their license: Okay, so we'll be a bank. Then what do we do?

But still. Duke and Ali would like DNB to get on with their decision. To them bunq partially consists of things that DNB can simply tick off their list based on the submitted paperwork. For the other part, DNB should have a live demonstration of what the app actually looks like to develop a more accurate feeling towards them. They believe a short demonstration would say more than eight hundred pages of paperwork.

They send an email with a link to a funny interpretation of 'Get Lucky', an overplayed summer hit, to try and wangle an invitation from DNB. It may not work, but it beats doing nothing, because doing nothing makes them uneasy.

To keep morale up, Ali suggests a retreat: three days of rest in the Ardennes as a reward for the uninterrupted toil and to help distract everyone from the wait.

At the edge of the village of Vielsalm, a large old villa is rented out for a haggled-down price. It comes with a fireplace big enough to stand in, a tennis court and enormous grounds with a phenomenal view. Nearly all of the bunqers are present: seventeen boys, one young woman and their brand new CFRO, although he only shows up for the first day.

Long, bunqer from day one, who left the company a few days prior to the trip, is also part of the crowd. Everyone's upset by the departure of their 'favorite Chinaman', as he calls himself. But the 'Cleareans', as he insists on calling them, understand his choice. Alongside his work for bunq, he's finally finished his studies and now he wants a job to match.

Sitting by the blazing fire, Djoeri mentions that this is the first time they've really relaxed. They haven't been able to see past the filing of the application. The process consisted of sprint after sprint, without knowing how long the race was.

The next morning, Duke and Jordi head for the tennis court; others spend the day swimming, mountain biking or hiking. Daan turns out be a true chef and takes charge of the kitchen in the evening. He even manages to get some bunqers to try their hand at cooking for the first time.

For a moment, they're distracted from the sluggishness of reality. On day three, however, the buzz returns. Vielsalm becomes a place of food, drink and debates about the future. Their plan is so good, so innovative, cutting-edge, intelligent and well-structured that DNB is probably in the process of deciding to ignore the 'concept' prefix and move onto instant consent. That should explain the delay.

On the way back, everyone's ready: bring on the future, we're all outta patience!

But the universe is not easily rushed.

The brand new CFRO arrives late for his first day. People who turn up late without a valid reason or screw up in some other way are supposed to treat the office to 'fail cake'. It's a bunq tradition, brought over from TransIP, which is covered in the handbook as well as in the introduction. The CFRO received both.

Considering the difference in background, the CFRO has been asked to pay extra attention to his exemplary role as a member of the Management Board, especially in terms of company culture. Bringing cake is a way of admitting guilt and acknowledging failure in order to move on as a team.

The CFRO, however, is not playing along. Instead, he sits down at the desk arranged for him and he waits. For what or whom remains unclear. The difference in culture between him and the two other members turns out to be enormous. It reminds Ali of a scene from the film 'Men in Black', with himself starring as Edwards, played by Will Smith.

Edwards: Maybe you already answered this question, but, why exactly are we here?

> *Jenson*: Second Lieutenant, Jake Jenson. West Point. Graduated with honors. We're here because you are looking for the best of the best of the best, sir!
> *Edwards*: Boy, Captain America over here! 'Best of the best of the best, sir! With honors.' Yeah, he's just really excited and he has no clue why we're here.

Within a week, patience has run out on all sides. The CFRO indeed has no idea what he's doing here with this gang of escaped teenagers. This isn't a serious bank, is it?

Daan, who deals with him directly, complains about his pace of thought during their conversations. His 'superior' has spent five full working days on reflection and none on actual production.

'Told you so,' Duke says without a hint of glee.

'OK, you were totally right,' Ali admits, aware — to his own reluctance — that he is bound to a copper handshake.

He immediately calls Candidate One, who vividly recalls their previous conversation and happily mentions that his assignment at RBS is nearly finished. On the downside, he's about to get on a plane bound for Thailand.

Ali asks to meet him at Schiphol Airport, but that turns out to be too tricky. They settle for a Skype call upon arrival, in about thirteen hours.

Ali brings him up to speed on his fall and its ongoing consequences. After fifteen minutes, a hot pain sears through his brain. A few minutes later, the power in Thailand cuts out.

It was enough. The second interview, conducted three weeks later by Docters van Leeuwen, confirms the impression Duke and Ali had and vice versa. Win.

The new CFRO, Pieter van der Harst, agrees to sign on his birthday: November 19th 2013.

From the beginning, there had been concerns about keeping the heart and soul of their movement intact. As they move from an innovative start-up into the financial world, they risk being contaminated by a culture of profits and bonuses. Guys like Attila and Daan consider themselves the core of the company. They want it to stay healthy, free of the virus that had its hold on the banking world since the 1980s.

There's no question about Docters van Leeuwen. He was one of the financial system's watchdogs for years. He wants bunq to instigate change. Besides, as a commissioner, he's a background figure.

However, they'll be dealing with Pieter van der Harst on a daily basis. Duke and Ali may consider him their intellectual equal and a match in character, a friendly finance guy with a soul and a conscience, but with three decades as a top banker, he's as good as fused with the system.

Pieter is part of banking history. During the 90s, he was director of financial markets at Banque de Suez, bought up in 1996 by SNS bank. Between 2010 and 2013 he worked for RBS on the dismantling of acquired ABN Amro leftovers. He was right at the tip of everything that's wrong with banks. And so they decide to take him out to dinner.

'RBS may have been the greatest corporate incident in the world of banking, but at least we started clearing up the mess before the others did,' says Pieter. 'Banks are oversized. In a healthy economy, the size of the banking sector should be no more than two or three percent of the total economy. In the Netherlands and the UK it's seven percent. Banks have also started going way too far beyond their core function. Besides, they have the capacity to greatly overpay for talents, which they're keeping away from the actual economy, and who subsequently end up using their talents to increase their own bonuses.'

Just like the regulators, Pieter wants more self-regulation, limits on variable remuneration and a separation of the consumer market and the business market. For all of the reasons mentioned, he thinks banks should focus on one thing: downsizing.

'However,' he continues, 'most banks have done the exact opposite by merging. In future, they'll want to merge even further, in a form of perceived self-defense. It's the only thing that will get them through the rat race they've created.'

Like Duke, Pieter found each bank he worked at to resemble a ministry: instead of focusing on enterprise or clients, they're looking out for themselves and other ministries/banks.

He sees how banks are split between their own usefulness and the greed of the market. Banks should be providing a safe place for clients to store their savings. This should include efficient payments – which, in his opinion, could be a lot more efficient. Efficient payments lead to trust, and trust is good for a modern economy.

It's a bank's job to make sure that money, the grease that keeps the wheels of the economy turning, can be safely stored and exchanged. Hence the temptation to regulate the sector. But for a long time, that regulation prevented healthy competition by newcomers, and because of this comfortable position of oligopoly, greed managed to take over, resulting in crises of trust, with devastating effects.

Pieter thinks that too little has been done to regain trust after 2008. 'Banks will either reinvent themselves, or disappear altogether. Neither DNB nor society want that to happen, so the banks will change.' he continues. 'Eventually, they'll have to do something about the complicated infrastructure and the high costs. They should have done so twenty years ago. They will set up a new system alongside the existing tangle of systems. They'll keep their clientele, but even that will disappear within a few decades.'

The financial system doesn't seem to have crushed Pieter's integrity. He passes the inquisition with flying colors.

Pieter's arrival kick starts discussions between Duke and Ali about what to expect once they have their license. They explore two extreme scenarios.

The negative scenario is that, as a newcomer, their concept threatens the established order. The financial world will resist bunq because it undermines existing structures.

The positive one is that bunq is neither a threat to, nor a solution for, the banking problem. Payments are such a small part of the money industry that there will be no resistance.

Duke and Ali hope that their true sting is in the change of paradigm, as they mentioned in their letter to Docters van Leeuwen. bunq as proof of concept. A manifestation of something that sounds like a crazy fantasy, but which proves that doing a better job is possible. If one party achieves success by reasoning from the point of view of the client and society, the model is bound to sell itself. Then, the banks will be in trouble. It's already happening with a number of mechanisms thought up by non-bankers, like crowdfunding and companies selling their bonds in order to finance themselves.

New legislation is cropping up that gives them hope. In 2010, Economist Paul Volcker, former chairman of the Economic Recovery Advisory Board under President Obama, proposed a law that should make it harder for banks to take risks. In the future, they will not be allowed to act purely for the sake of financial gain. Instead, they will have to be able to prove a connection between their products and the needs of their clients. In terms of hedging (the covering of an investment risk by making another investment) he wants the risks to be specific, identifiable and defined.

With Obama's support, the bill has since been running through the maze of amendments and lobbies, and will soon be put before the five federal supervisors who make the final decision. Passing the so-called 'Volcker Rule' would result in great reform for the American banking sector.

And a vital one too, because without reform, a new financial crisis is only matter of time, Docters van Leeuwen predicts. 'And this time, it will go really fast.' Some banking products are, as investor and philanthropist Warren Buffett puts it, financial weapons of mass destruction.

Frustration Flaring Up

Six weeks after the conceptual application there's still no word from DNB. In the meantime, the competition is beginning to make some bunqers nervous.

One thousand inhabitants of the city of Leiden, as well as roughly one-hundred-and-fifty local shops, are taking part in an experiment conducted by ING, Rabobank and ABN Amro: paying with your smartphone, without a PIN code. The guinea pigs all receive a special mobile phone fitted with a Near Field Communication (NFC) chip. In order to make a payment, you hold the device close to a payment machine. After the trial period, the subjects get to keep the phone. The smartphone itself is a bit of a drawback, as it's difficult to put on the market on a large scale, explains a spokesperson.

The test in Leiden is supposed to undercut credit card giant Visa. They, too, are developing the use of mobile phones for transactions. Besides that, ABN Amro has been talking about an app for sharing and calculating joint payments based on email addresses. The app allows you to send a payment request with an explanation and provides an overview of who has paid, etc.

To top it off, PayPal is launching the Beacon. Or at least, announcing it. The PayPal Beacon — a physical device to use in shops — connects to the customer's phone using Bluetooth. Customers pay by checking into the business. It can work automatically or by confirming your purchase in the PayPal app. A profile photo lets the shopkeeper know that the real customer is standing in front of them.

Although bunq's ideas are much more innovative, the threatening progress from others does leave a lot to think about. There's nothing they can do about it either, because they're stuck waiting on the DNB to make a decision.

They try to dispel each other's unease by pointing out that the competition is stuck in old systems like the wallet, the top-up chip card or NFC, and that they all require investments into hardware from the pre-internet era. They're stuffing old programs with new complexities, so goes the mantra.

The initiatives all seem to fizzle out quite quickly, but they increase the feeling of urgency at bunq. It's only once they have a permit that they can really begin their innovation, the half-baked solutions can be swept aside and the games can begin. Why is DNB so unbelievably slow?

Because it's the supervisor's role to be thorough and methodical. The pile of documents is examined systematically and in numeric order. From one, to two, to three... Then, once the bottom of the pile has been reached and it's cleared to move onto the next level, the whole process starts again from one, to two, to three... The people aren't the problem, the unfamiliarity with the process is.

The level of detail at each stage is preventing DNB from performing an overall, conceptual assessment. bunq may be 'up all night to get lucky', but the top dogs at DNB, who just might be welcoming their plan and speeding up the process, are still blissfully ignorant whilst the lower echelons take ages to sift through all kinds of details.

Every day, someone in Team Overhead throws themselves at the pile of newly-delivered mail, only to return to work in frustration. Seven full weeks after handing in the conceptual application, Duke finally recognizes the DNB logo. 'Guys!' They huddle around the envelope, from which Daan triumphantly pulls a stack of paperwork...

Containing twenty-three pages filled with questions about practically everything.

There is little appreciation for the supervisor's thorough approach.

'DNB doesn't get it,' rages Daan as he goes through the questions. 'These people can't see past the banking world as it is now: overcomplicated and as expensive as possible. What's so difficult to understand about a simple bank that only does payments? If you can't even understand that, how clueless are you?' Djoeri loses it over an investment condition: 'Someone finally tries to be risk free, but no! They bring up "investments to increase profit"!'

'For fuck's sake, seriously?' Ali vents. A cluster of questions seem to imply that DNB thinks bunq will be offering a savings account, and suggesting that zero percent is quite a low interest rate. Which is precisely the opposite of what they're trying to do. Besides that, despite the long preparation time, the document is riddled with typos and other inaccuracies. 'Are we supposed to take all of these twenty-three pages seriously? Are we expected to actually reward each ridiculous question with an elaborate answer?'

At the end of the day, bunq settles down. They've been unsuccessful in getting DNB to understand the kind of bank they want to become and what they want to do. What, or who, needs to change?

In the meantime, that same week, *Blown Away* appears, a

bundle of twenty-eight poems by Docters van Leeuwen.

You are no sleeping beauty
As you lie in your display
Shrunken black and grayish rags
Cover your shriveled frame

Yet something unbinds you
Broad jaws, that still reveal
– beyond the usual grin of death –
A salacious smile like butter, tall yellow grass

Like a relic of lushness, of lust
You fill this translucent grave
A devourer of men who died of diarrhea
But nevertheless a victress
Fleeting and triumphant.
– From: 'De Deense dode' (the Danish dead) –

Shortly after the publication of *Blown Away*, the Dutch themselves are blown away during the great storm of October 2013. With gale force winds of over 60 mph, it's the strongest storm in over 23 years. Trains are delayed. bunqers on their bicycles struggle in vain against the raging winds that make the towers in the city shake.

Still wrestling with their disappointment and with little enthusiasm left to get them through the all-nighters, bunq pulls itself together.

Duke and Ali rally the troops and compose a battle plan in order to respond to the twenty-three question-filled pages as soon as possible. What choice do they have?

Again, hectic weeks follow.

Exactly two months after the cold shower of questions, on November 26, 2013, the final application is sent off. DNB now officially has thirteen weeks of ‘regulation time’ to respond: next to the pile of documents is a chess clock, which is stopped whenever a question comes up. It’s only restarted when they receive a satisfactory answer from bunq.

Feverish games of chess are being played on other boards, too. The federal regulators’ clock in the United States is ticking. With a time difference of six to eleven hours depending on the time zone, the Volcker Rule is passed on December 11, 2013. Immediately afterwards, a number of smaller American banks countermove by filing a legal appeal against the new law.

In the Netherlands, Minister of Finance Jeroen Dijsselbloem announces steps to prevent excess in the banking culture. In two years, as of 2015, there will be a cap on bonuses in the financial sector.

The banks respond swiftly and effectively. State-owned bank ABN Amro immediately raises their top managers’ fixed salaries by almost twenty percent, preemptively compensating for any threat of capped bonuses. Top dog and former Minister of Finance Gerrit Zalm emphasizes that it concerns only a ‘handful’ of people. Besides, it’s not a raise, but really a salary cut, as he explains to the press. The bonus was a variable remuneration of 50 percent, the standard pay is only being raised by 16.7 percent, which is much less, really. Or so he claims.

Something similar happens abroad. The mega-banks

come up with monthly allowances to get around the internationally agreed caps. The top executive at Goldman Sachs, for example, rakes in some 14.1 million euros extra each year. That's over a million euros of additional income per month. The combined bonuses at Goldman Sachs, Bank of America, Morgan Stanley, JP Morgan Chase and Citigroup total over one billion euros, and is divided among a group of people too small to fill a Boeing 747.

British bank Barclays announces that they will be cutting twelve thousand jobs: profits are 32 percent lower than the previous year. But they don't let that spoil the fun: management receives a 10 percent increase in bonuses, the corporate branch even gets 13 percent. The increase is vital to remain attractive to talented bankers — claim the talented bankers.

In short: 2013 does not go down in history as the year of repentance and innovation. The banks can sit back and wait for the storm of indignation to die down as usual. And bunq can start packing.

EXHAUSTION

Catch-22

On December 1, 2013, bunq moves half a mile north to a new view across from a muddy building site: Orly Square.

Stacks of freight containers and tall fences block the road. It looks like a wasteland. The traffic primarily consists of diggers, heavy-booted builders, drug dealers and the odd office worker. Confused tourists make their way across a sloppy arrangement of plank bridges. This, according to Google Maps, is where their hotel should be. In disbelief and bad English, they ask for directions. Like bunq, Orly Square has plenty of room to grow into something better than it is today.

The new office consists of a single, deserted floor. A sea-greenish carpet with orange lines runs from window to window in musty, worn out tracks. The few remaining plasterboard walls can be pierced with a finger – in so far as this hasn't already been done.

The walls are knocked down, the bunqers rip the carpet out and the floor gets a coat of paint. Roos, Djoeri and a big group of fellow bunqers drag their furniture and equipment to the new building in a rental van. The move is scheduled for Friday evening and Saturday so it doesn't interfere with the working week. Some items don't fit into the elevator, not even after they lift out the ceiling. They are dragged up five flights of stairs from the parking garage. They manage to source the last bits and pieces at a bankruptcy sale.

Roos, 24 years old, joined bunq a few weeks ago. Before that she had worked at Michael Page, a recruitment agency.

It was a tough lesson in recruitment. She's not afraid of the deep end or to get her hands dirty. She moves mountains with a constant smile on her face.

Straight after the weekend, everyone is back to work. They are sitting at the end of the large open space: the canteen. While they work, builders are clicking partitions onto strips, creating a light and spacious corridor with transparent offices on either side. Only a small percentage of the space is fitted out with a table and desktop: the new office was rented with the future in mind.

They decide to have a joint Christmas party with TransIP in the newly refurbished accommodation. The event doubles up as a housewarming. As they close off their newly created workspaces, everyone huddles together in the canteen for the 'rave'. A tipsy TransIPer performs a table dance just after midnight, sending glasses flying in every direction.

Djoeri, with his 'dual nationality', notices how despite their shared DNA, bunqers and TransIPers aren't really mingling. Perhaps it's the difference in phases. bunqers spend their time in constant battle and insecurity, lurched back and forth between hope and disappointment. TransIPers are filled with confidence at their proven success, looking to the future with positivity in anticipation of even more victories.

Barely one week into 2014, while the mess of the housewarming party is still being cleaned up, Ali enters Attila's new office.

'I think we need to simplify,' he says. He means the code.

It's been nearly a year since Ali threw their first months of programming out with the trash. A few months of non-stop programming later, Scala was scrapped. They rebuilt the new foundation from scratch in PHP, and built up from that.

But Ali is still unsatisfied. Like writing, coding is deleting. The ideal coder manages to convey the message through a minimal set of words that paint a clear image. Most importantly, a coder has to strive for clarity. If he wants to build something complex, he's better off avoiding long sentences, with lots of by-sentences, commas and other constructs that are difficult to read. He should split the work into multiple, smaller chunks. According to Ali, the clarity in the code is not sufficiently there. He takes Attila through an architectural preview of the elements that need improving or simplification. It amounts to a lot.

Each user, for example, has the option of storing data in their own database. This prevents the main database from becoming too large. Also, it offers users the option of storing their data in the Netherlands only, using a personal data code or encryption key.

It's a fundamental crown jewel: completely decentralized banking, without going through an umbrella organization, system or bank that oversees the transactions. Simply move your money directly from your own 'money database' into someone else's using your smartphone, without intervention from a third party.

It's so revolutionary and so far ahead of its time that even the in-house crowd finds it hard to comprehend.

The coders have tried to make the architecture as future-proof as possible, but they wanted too much too quickly. It's called 'feature creep': the constant addition of new features, with more and more creeping in unnoticed. 'Since, while we're at it, wouldn't it be great if... Because it could be, and imagine if later on...' The code ends up lost in a self-imposed maze of 'just in case one day' — demands.

They need to take a step back and create something simple and flawless, and then expand as and when necessary. Set it up simply rather than over-engineer.

To Ali, there's only one possible conclusion. Again, several months worth of work is shoved into the virtual shredder.

For Pieter, too, the year could not have got off to a worse start. The financial director and natural optimist is physically shaking. He's just received a stack of redirected mail from the old office. There's a letter with the message that DNB has no faith in the venture. Dazed, he checks the date. The fatal note was sent just before Christmas. Despite the moving notice, sent in ample time, the letter was still sent to the wrong address.

Pieter reads it again, his hands trembling. His years of experience have taught him that DNB always takes a formal, legal stance in writing. He's never yet had a letter from them that hasn't given him a mild stomach ache. But this one's more like a sucker punch to the gut.

Ever since his arrival at bunq, six weeks ago, he's been absolutely convinced that they will get their license. On his first day they gave him a wooden abacus as a birthday gift: an old-fashioned wooden calculating frame, with a hand-made inscription: 'be basic — be bunq'. bunq is basic. The concept and the risk profile are so clear, so simple that the supervisor should have no choice but to grant them the permit. Even if DNB didn't want to, they could never refuse. bunq's concept poses no formal or legal risk from DNB's perspective.

'DNB thinks the viability of our company hasn't been sufficiently proven,' Pieter paraphrases to his fellow managers. He finds it incomprehensible. The plan and the business model are solid. Besides, the question of whether bunq is successful shouldn't matter to DNB, as long as there's sufficient capital to tie up all loose ends in the event of failure – which there is. Their contacts at DNB, the market access guys, agreed with them on that. And they still do.

Still, says DNB: you can already make mobile phone payments with ABN Amro, right?

The bunqers rack their brains over why they're failing to convey the essence of their concept. Is it a simple question of points of reference, different characters? Are they so different that even the simplest explanation becomes the most complicated?

Whenever bunq tries to sketch an image for the future, DNB responds with a number. Research, they say, shows that people only have 2.5 bank accounts on average and find it difficult to open a new one.

'We don't want people to open a new account, we want them to open up to a new world,' Ali responds. 'See Spotify, see Tesla. Excel fetishists are per definition not in a position to comment on the success of a completely novel concept!'

Completely novel? Suddenly, it dawns on him. You can indeed pay by phone with ABN Amro. In that sense, bunq isn't entirely new. Their payment app, however, is significantly faster, better and more fun than any other bank's. And the app will continue to develop relentlessly quickly compared to those of the original banks. So bunq doesn't need to compete with new banks: in the future, everyone will use bunq on the side, like a WhatsApp for transactions!

The only way of bridging the lack of understanding at DNB is to show them the app. A completely new interpretation of the word 'bank' can't be explained, it needs to be experienced.

Pieter immediately gets in touch with his contact at DNB to ask whether they can finally demonstrate the app. The request has been made many times before in vain, but this time... DNB says yes!

Is it because the request comes from Pieter, the man with the history in banking? Could some continuous stream of miscommunications have been the cause of the lack of understanding? Regardless: the meeting is set in two weeks time, on January 17.

Because bunq is new and Duke and Ali lack a track record, Pieter knows that their main challenge will be to speak the language of the supervisor. He sets up the presentation following a structure DNB uses internally, adhering to their format and step-by-step thought process.

For example, DNB first assesses a business model by its strategy, then by the main drivers of income, the risks, et cetera, until they've determined the viability. Much will depend on what DNB recognizes as truly novel.

Armed with a few crucial pointers from Docters van Leeuwen, and after Sergey's checked, double-checked and triple-checked the demo, the three bunqeteers and their lawyer Casper set off to DNB.

They're kitted out with laptops and mobile phones. Ali has squeezed himself into a suit as he did for the introductory meeting. Although that was over six months ago, he still struggles with concentration and exhaustion. The first won't return, the other won't go.

Five critical members of the supervision team sit across the table from them as Pieter kicks off with numbers and prognoses. The theme is 'bunq as an innovative service', but he focuses on the risks, which are limited for DNB. Why hold back an innovation of this magnitude if the financial risks in the event of failure are non-existent?

Again, DNB bangs on about crediting, currently a combination of government bonds and crowdfunding. DNB does not want any crowdfunding, but it turns out they're open to investment in government bonds – under certain conditions, yet to be specified.

Ali demonstrates the app, which goes very smoothly. The men in the supervision team show signs of understanding, but no enthusiasm. Casper doesn't even need to open his mouth.

Three uncertain weeks after the demonstration, on February 6, 2014, DNB finally sends the minutes from the meeting including a list of bullet points they want to see clarified.

Pieter and Jordi throw themselves at the questions and return the answers within a week. From that moment onwards, it's back to regulation time: DNB legally has six weeks to respond.

It means, Duke works out, that they won't be getting a definitive answer before April. And that means Duke is forced to return to their potential clients with yet another message of delay.

bunq is stuck in a four-point Catch-22. The code has been discarded, the programming started afresh. The work continues until eyes redden and night falls. Sensors in the programming offices switch off the lights if they don't detect movement for half an hour. It happens nearly every thirty minutes. The coders are motionless when they work — only their fingers flash across their keyboards.

They're coding in the dark, literally and figuratively. Transactions between banks have to go through a clearing & settlement agency, via the European Central Bank (ECB). This agency opens the door to debit cards, credit cards and other links in the transaction chain. If you transfer money from one bank to another, the system sends a message. These messages and the corresponding amounts are subsequently added up for all banks and settled internally: 'the settlement'. This all happens through the so-called Target2 network: an account that each bank has at the ECB.

In order to develop functional modules that are able to communicate with the existing transactional infrastructure, they need to know its data and specifications. However, bunq can only access this sensitive data if it's hooked up to such a clearing & settlement agency, which of course requires... a banking license. Only once they have access to the connections within the network, can the coders actually begin to develop the programs and tests that make the connections work.

But DNB won't lend a permit until they've had the quality and safety of the IT systems tested by their own people, and until there's a clear demand in the market.

The business community is showing interest, but the uncertainty in the progress is getting in the way of actual business deals. At the same time, DNB wants to see signed agreements in order to be able to assess the viability of the business case.

Everything is either interdependent or conflicting. Business development is waiting for IT, IT is waiting for the permit, and the permit is dependent on both business development and IT.

The whole thing creates a feeling of powerlessness and irritability in the office. Supposed lack of understanding or willingness from DNB provides a mutual vent, but mostly it feeds a common uncertainty. Just as tourists find it hard to believe in the alluring oasis of their hotel, so do some of the bunqers as they begin to think their vision is more of a fantasy after all.

When it comes to DNB, bunq is forced to be the reactive and dependent party, and the difference in response time is enormous.

bunq is a group of freebooters. They have complete self-determination. Any minor step DNB might want to take involves a complete overhaul of policy. Besides, DNB is in transition. Half of the activities and staff are in the process of moving to Frankfurt, to take over the supervision of major banks.

If bunq still wants to launch its app in 2014 — over a years' worth of cost and competition later than originally planned — the permit will need to be in by September at the latest. How can they break the status quo and speed the dragging process up?

Duke, Ali and Pieter each go through the contact lists on their phones. Since the very beginning, Duke and Ali have freed up a lot of time for networking. As banking rookies, they understand that having friends in high places is a bonus, and information always becomes of use sooner or later.

Scrolling through his contacts faster than the average teenager, it dawns on Pieter that his former colleague Jeroen Kremers, with whom he worked at RBS, might be available as he also finished his work at RBS.

In 2011, Kremers was one of three possible successors for Nout Wellink as president of DNB. His background at the Ministry of Finance, as founder of the Dutch supervisory model at the AFM and his directorship of the International Monetary Fund (IMF) made him an extremely suitable candidate. But the job went to Klaas Knot, the fourth man. Kremers then chose to carry out the socially significant task of cleaning up the mess at RBS as Chief Risk Officer.

Ali and Duke have spoken to him before. In that conversation, despite Kremers' background being entirely different to theirs, they detected an urge for innovation. They probed him for a role as commissioner, but he refused at the time. His tasks at RBS simply took up too much of his time. He was, however, available as a sounding board and intermediary, if need be.

They realize that this is the moment to ask again.

During their conversation, Kremers immediately notices that bunq is still very clear on what they don't want: to be a classical bank. It's a more mellow version of the anti-bank attitude that was so abundant at the beginning of the start-up. Their fresh idea of bunq as a

WhatsApp-for-transactions obviously hasn't cured them of their anti-bank sentiments.

Kremers believes their profiling themselves as anti-bank is exactly what's holding them back from being positively convincing. He also finds the attitude too simplistic. It's not helping his conversation partners. He would like them to work with what they do want. A constructive attitude enforces innovation and will inevitably lead to something special.

It inspires him. Besides, he's quite excited at the prospect of reuniting with two former colleagues he highly values: Docters van Leeuwen from his days at AFM, and Pieter, from RBS. He decides to accept.

On March 27, 2014, a reliable rumor makes its way through the grapevine from DNB, suggesting that the case manager will be issuing a positive advice. If it's true, DNB's methodical procedure could, for the first time, work in their favor.

In DNB's tiered levels of responsibility, a positive internal advice nearly always leads to approval, as all internal tuning and agreement has already taken place beforehand. The definitive 'yes' is just a matter of time.

The question however is: how much time?

Inner Circle III: *Deadline*

The third Inner Circle takes place on March 31, 2014. As CEO, Ali introduces the official bodies to the slightly increased group of friends, contacts and interested parties. This time they have Pieter as their financial director and Jeroen Kremers as their fourth member of the Supervisory Board.

Using a timeline, he tries to convince the Inner Circle members, and maybe more so the attending bunqers, that there's light at the end of the lengthy DNB tunnel. If DNB sticks to its own rule book, their deadline will pass in four or five days.

The bank license time line

November 25, 2013	License request sent
December 23, 2013	Letter from DNB
January 17, 2014	Meeting with DNB
January 22, 2014	Letter from DNB
January 28, 2014	Response sent
March 2014	Informal contact
March 3, 2014	Additional information sent
March 2014	More informal contact
March 19-24, 2014	Further information sent
Early April	Deadline

Looking beyond the deadline, Duke presents the expansion of their business development team, explaining the importance of the retail and hospitality industries to their business model.

Users want to be able to transfer money to each other, but also make payments to companies. That's why they need launching partners: companies willing to use bunq as a payment system from day one. Ever since the Minister of Traffic and Water Management made her first debit card payment at a petrol station in 1985, even the smallest companies have been forced to invest in the hardware required for that payment system. bunq cuts away those costs: if you own a tablet, you own a cash register.

Duke explains that he has a hit list of roughly five hundred targets. He also introduces his latest addition to the team. A month ago, David joined them. He's a well-groomed, clever 27-year-old with a good heart. In a frat-boyish way, he's both streetwise and dead honest.

His meeting with Duke and Ali gave him an instant buzz. He appreciates their confidence, shocking directness and work pace, not to mention the fact that they're working on huge, innovative stuff.

The meeting took place on a Friday. On the following Monday, he ends his career at Henkel. He didn't realize until later that the project was about founding a new kind of bank.

Andrew Citroen is also in the room. A prior pillar of support for Duke, he's the third in a line of directors at family firm Cikam. Set up in 1945 as an office machines sales company, the firm is now best known as a cash processor. Wherever cash is exchanged, Cikam looks after its 'depositing, sorting, recirculation, counting and checking'. bunq wants to turn this cash world into a cashless society. Strangely, Andrew 'Lemon' Citroen is pleased about that.

With his cufflinks made from old quarters, his tanned face and slick hair combed back, his navy suit and a Rolex on his wrist, he looks like he's just walked off the set of *La Dolce Vita*. He thinks bunq will set off a bomb under all payment traffic. Why is a cash man like him such a fan of that notion?

The Association of Dutch Banks has a ten-year goal of balancing out the cash/electronic payment ratio at 55/45. Cash remains dominant: especially because of the circulation of black money and the tourism sector. But Andrew is convinced that the payment landscape, as well as its players, will do a full 180 in the coming years: less cash, more electronic payments.

If the world is changing, you'd better not be caught on the sidelines. So Andrew brought bunq to the attention of some of his major clients. He's shown clients the demo, but the app turns out to have changed on several occasions, forcing him to make an embarrassed and annoyed phone call to Duke.

Duke's hit list consists of the names of managers and owners who are open to innovation. It also includes companies that combine physical shops with online ones. Some of them were brought in by Andrew.

A few of those on the list are present at the meeting. The 'early April' message might just allow bunq to get these companies – and several smaller ones – on board. But they're wondering whether April is realistic.

Ali's closing lines directly address these concerns: 'Realistic expectations lead to realistic results. But realism doesn't change the world. Dreams do'.

In the Media

At the end of the first week of April there's still no word from DNB, let alone a permit. Regulation time is a clear concept, but if you can't see the other person's clock... By continuing to bring up questions, DNB can stretch their time frame as much as they like.

Pieter's annoyance at the lack of transparency in the process and the effort it takes him to get hold of his contact is growing by the minute. The so-called direct line is usually put through to the secretary's office, where they promise to pass on the message. Then nothing happens for ages. Pieter calls again and ends up right back at the secretary's office.

His persistence has already caused irritation once. Casper-the-lawyer is tipped off that Pieter is too hot on the DNB's heels. He's too pushy. A stalker. Casper is to convey the following message to him: 'phoning three times a day is not going to help.' Pieter then finds out that if you phone just after 5 pm, you get connected through to the reception, which then often connects you straight to the mobile number of the person you're after. Unfortunately the leak is quickly sealed.

In order to de-escalate the situation, Pieter makes an informal deal with DNB about the regularity of contact, so that both parties stay up-to-date on any developments. It may not be progress, but it saves a lot of frustration.

As an experienced veteran, Sergey describes the atmosphere amongst the coders. It's not just the endless and seemingly pointless programming that's getting to them, but the insecurity about the banking license, too.

'In a start-up, nothing is clear. Decisions about the app or even the future of the company can be taken in the space of five minutes. Whether DNB consents or not, the future's still unclear. You never know what other banks are going to do. We're only a small company and an obstructive colleague is easily gotten rid of. In Russia, anyway.'

Jeroen Kremers is soon party to the continuing insecurity. He, too, thinks that bunq meets every formal requirement. But apparently DNB is still insufficiently convinced of the material side of things. He appeals to the bunqers to keep faith in the permit.

Ali deals with the issue differently. Why doesn't DNB just do what they're legally supposed to? In other words, reach a verdict within the set time frame and guidelines? He guesses the supervisor is delaying over a subjective assessment. DNB's main legal task is to calculate risks. And that's exactly the part that bunq's covered really well with their start-up capital and pre-financed settlement plan. It's not even been an issue in any of their conversations with DNB.

The more Ali's expectations are tried, the more persistent he becomes. One way or another, it will happen! His conviction is solid as a rock, and despite their impatience and frustration, the other bunqers hang onto it for dear life.

On May 7, 2014, *het Financieele Dagblad* (*Dutch Financial Times*) publishes an interview with the heading 'Adapt size of bank to European market'. The article is about the role banks have in financing the economy. It highlights a problem, mainly regarding small and medium enterprises. Top banker Kremers has been asked for solutions. One of those is to stimulate more new blood in the banking market.

'DNB has indicated that the Dutch banking market is highly concentrated. We can avoid this by attracting more newcomers into that market. I'm an advisor to a group of young entrepreneurs who are looking to start a new bank. The large number of rules and regulations prove to be a high barrier to entry.'

A few pages later, Jeroen pops up again under the heading: 'New bank struggling to get off the ground'. The article says that the government should do more to stimulate innovation in the banking sector. The credit flow needs to get going again and that requires new players in the market. 'However, at the moment, it's very difficult to get new initiatives underway in the financial sector'.

The piece continues with a warning of large changes in earning models. 'It would be a great shame if the Brits or the Germans ended up writing history, because their innovations beat us to it.'

The next day, an editorial piece completes the hat trick.

NEW BANK DESERVES A CHANCE

DNB faces a dilemma. The supervisor is pro-competition in the banking sector. The Dutch market is ruled by three large banks and such density in the market creates a negative impact on market forces. At the same time, DNB is responsible for the safeguarding of financial stability, which means placing tough demands on the attainment of a bank permit.

> For a group of young entrepreneurs from the IT sector, the threshold is so high that it's getting in the way of their initiative to start a new bank. They're unlucky enough to want to innovate in a time of new regulations to the sector, which in themselves serve a good purpose: increasing financial stability.
>
> Perhaps there's a way, without undermining the demands, to differentiate between different kinds of banking permits. If the bank starts out with payment traffic only, then the demands could be lower than for a bank that starts out with extensive lending. The new bank could 'grow into' a full permit as time goes on. Also, the discussion about the new bank should prompt the government and supervisory bodies to consider the structure of the financial market. Healthy competition, nationally and internationally, will pave the way for innovations which may prove useful to the European market. (Source: *het Financieele Dagblad*)

At Orly Square, everyone gathers in excitement. Ali stresses that all secrecy is still intact.

Although he's happy with the media coup, he's annoyed at the passage about different kinds of banking permits. They're not at all in favor of differentiation on that front, and certainly not some 'diet' license. However small bunq is, they fully comply with all legal requirements, just like the big boys. All they want is for DNB to hurry up and approve.

Before 9 am on May 7, the day of the first article, DNB's case officer is on the line with a sincere: 'Congratulations on the good press'. It's the first time anyone from the supervisor's office has picked up a phone on their own accord.

On the day of the large newspaper spread, an email follows: people 'higher up' in DNB have asked after the business case.

Duke and Ali credit the acceleration at DNB directly to the articles in *het Financieele Dagblad*. Pieter calls it a coincidence: 'No letter at DNB is written in a day.' He does, however, think that the attention from the press will increase the pressure on DNB: 'They won't want to be accused of holding back innovation.'

Jeroen himself is happy to conclude that the top levels of control at DNB are showing interest in bunq. He's also suddenly swamped with phone calls from parties that are also working on something new.

Nearly simultaneously, Jeroen ends up on the news himself, along with Pieter. bunq too is mentioned by name:

> **EX-RBS BANKERS RECEIVE OVER ONE MILLION IN LUMP SUMS**
> Top bankers Jeroen Kremers and Pieter van der Harst cashed in sizeable lump sum payments from the Dutch branch of RBS. The ex-leaders split almost 1.2 million euros between them. RBS Netherlands is one of three parts of what used to be ABN Amro (Source: RTL Z)

RTL Z continues the clip with a bit of banking history and speaks of 'leaving quietly through the back door', 'accomplished tasks' and 'voluntary redundancy schemes in keeping with the banking code'. The final sentence goes:

> As of the start of this year, Van der Harst (54) has been financial director at Bunq, a new automation company.

If you google 'bunq', you find Bunq.nl, an automation company. But Bunq is not bunq, as bunq keeps its activities classified. The scoop revolves around the wrong company. It takes weeks for bunq to buy the domain name, for a lot more than it would have cost them before all the commotion.

Ali's upset about the coverage. 'Cashing in and splitting sizeable lump sum payments' sounds dodgy.

He detests the tendency of certain media to exaggerate stories. They use facts in order to imply independent journalism and add suggestions to sell those facts. He openly defends Pieter. Is that not hypocritical?

Ali explains why he doesn't think so. He argues that Pieter was part of an unhealthy culture for a long time, but that his character allowed him to come out unscathed. He remained loyal to his task, up to the point of his own departure. Even when RBS was having a rough time, he didn't choose the easy way out.

'Do I have to defend Pieter?' Ali asks, rhetorically. 'No, but I do. It's a principle. If you start to make normal situations appear wrong, you lose nuance and any image of the sector becomes a parody. How, then, do you identify the things that are really wrong, and fix it?'

And the lump sum?

'Considerable on the face of it, but after fourteen years with the same employer, it's not excessive. Certainly not in banking terms. It's a lot less than elsewhere in the banking sector. More importantly: it allows Pieter to work here with us for a fraction of what he could earn elsewhere.'

In terms of his monthly salary, Pieter has settled for less than half of what he used to earn, and there are no bonuses. 'No one,' says Ali, 'can tell me that Pieter is greedy.'

When asked about it, Pieter just shrugs and resumes his work.

It's May 21, 2014, two weeks after their media hat trick, and music is playing in the canteen. Over two years after the accident, Ali can finally deal with slight levels of sound. His phone rings. He walks into the corridor and picks up. DNB.

He rushes into one of the glass offices and shuts the door. A meeting. The following month, on Friday the 13th, DNB wants to review the board. First Ali, then Duke, then Pieter, then the members of the Supervisory Board.

bunq celebrates it like a victory. They're another step closer — as is a certain semi-nonchalant thirty-something-year-old man later that day.

He sneaks through the door behind one of the bunqers, walks halfway into the canteen, past two of the four pillars that run along the corridor to the place where an old cash register stands, symbolizing bygone times. The bunqer turns around and asks: 'What are you doing here?'.

The man turns out to be an employee of ING Bank — trying to snoop around. It appears ING has a small unbranded office elsewhere in the building. This is news to many bunqers. In a few weeks, the man reveals, they'll be expanding to the fourth floor. Directly opposite of bunq.

Time to change the door policy. Dominik orders a finger scanner and everyone has to register their prints.

But that's not the end of it: for weeks on end, the elevator traffic is remarkably high. Whenever a bunqer takes the elevator, so does an INGer: 'So... that deadline of yours: did you guys make it in the end? The other day you told me about your project; what was it again? ...'

Double D-Days

The day of his review is nearly a full year after that of his first visit to DNB. Ali still feels like a completely different man: his body is easily tired, his mind is slow. His stamina is pretty much ruined. The worst thing is that his condition is holding bunq back, especially in terms of progression of the code: 'Real, permanent brain damage, lost time. Time our competitors are making good use of.'

Friday the 13th, the day of the review, holds up to its reputation by giving Ali a fever and a nasty cold. Despite his enmity towards it, he decides to take (loads of) paracetamol to get through the day.

In his mind, everything depends on this one day. This is where it all comes together. He's been unable to prepare properly. Partly because of his health, but mainly because no one could or would tell him what the contents of the review are, or what questions to expect. He's heard plenty of tall tales: supposedly it will resemble a police-like interrogation including a game of good cop, bad cop every now and then.

Ali sits down to face his interrogators and counts a fourth, unannounced, DNBer. Plus he gets confronted with the fact that there will be a second interview with him before he even says a word. Usually, or so he's heard, that only happens when there's a problem. So what's the reason for the second interview, he wonders? After all: he hadn't even opened his mouth yet.

The explanation soon follows. A single director who is

also the main shareholder, and not even from the banking world, is cause for extra caution: therefore, the leadership of DNB wants to meet him in person on Wednesday July 9, with a follow-up conversation with the sub-leadership about the structure of bunq.

A number of pre-filled competence and suitability matrixes form the basis of the actual review.

Duke, Pieter and Ali have put themselves and each other under a magnifying glass, both individually as well as collectively. In the forms, they've indicated strong and weak qualities and how they will compensate for their shortcomings. DNB prefers examples. Name a situation, for example, in which Ali's impatience has had a negative impact on bunq. And please explain how that was mitigated?

Not that he's currently impatient. He's too insecure and too dazed by his condition. But he's sound enough to struggle his way through the questions on a satisfactory level, at least for now.

Duke's review goes smoothly. The men speak each other's language, sympathize with each other, and Duke's background in the financial world suffices.

Pieter, familiar with DNB, experiences his review like a meet up with like-minded people. They grill him on the dynamics within the Board of Directors and ask whether the CEO is challenged when necessary. He confirms.

He uses the example of how ongoing discussions have caused a shift in the 'anti-bank attitude'. He, too, finds the attitude outdated.

The review requirement also applies to members of the Supervisory Board, who are yet to be formally appointed.

Docters van Leeuwen is forced to pass up on the invitation: he's been unwell for a while. Instead of an active sixty-something-year-old, he feels like an unfit old man. He's exhausted from a five-meter walk and has to recover before he's able to travel the next five. Heart failure, the doctors suspect. He no longer deems himself capable of properly fulfilling his role as a board member and withdraws. Jeroen Kremers will be acting chair.

While the other board members have long since received their invitations, Emiel Roozen hears nothing from DNB. He receives no clarification as to why this might be, which makes Roozen realize that his review could cause a major delay if things continue in this way. He too withdraws.

The sudden withdrawal of a single official, let alone two, is a dramatic turn: and so bunq scrambles to replace them as soon as possible. Fortunately they hit a bit of good luck.

For a week before Roozen withdraws, Ali and Pieter speak to the CEO and Chairman of RBS Netherlands, Jan de Ruiter. Pieter made the connection, suspecting that De Ruiter – who previously headed Equity Capital Markets and European Equity at ABN Amro – might be a very suitable member of the Inner Circle.

It's a lively conversation. Ali promises Jan to send him a copy of his book *Entrepreneurs never catch a break*. At home, he grabs him a copy and signs the first page: 'Happy to welcome you as an Inner Circle member'.

Still surprised at the turn of events that lost them Roozen, Pieter calls Jan back on Monday afternoon, with a new request. 'Would you be interested in helping us out? We have an urgent vacancy on the Supervisory Board ...' De Ruiter, already up to date on bunq's plans, says yes immediately. He deals with the formalities by Wednesday.

On Thursday he has permission from RBS — including a clause saying that the agreement will be subject to review if bunq ventures into the United Kingdom.

That night, Ali picks up the book that's still on his table. He finds a pen and makes a correction:

> 'Happy to welcome you as ~~an Inner Circle member~~ commissioner'

Meanwhile, in Orly Square, Daan makes a remarkable discovery. He finds brand new forms on the DNB website, all of which contain relevant information about the licensing process.

They appear to have been created, worded and adapted during the period in which bunq was in the dark about their application. Clearly bunq's input has been used as a source: the sweet irony makes him laugh uncontrollably. What a weird process indeed.

Ali's been free of fever for a week. But while he's counting his blessings, it turns out that the database – bunq's technological core – is riddled with programming faults. The IT team pulls several all-nighters to fix the issues one by one. Once that's done, Ali can finally start preparing for his second interview with DNB — or so he thinks.

He receives an unexpected call from a DNB secretary. They're asked to show their demo to DNB's leaders on the same day as the follow-up interview. A meeting to discuss bunq's structure will subsequently take place. The bunqers requested the demo-part and have finally succeeded in convincing DNB of its relevance... but three appointments in one day is a bit too much. They have no other option than to move demo-day forward.

With one day less to comb through the code and correct it, the pressure increases even further. Apparently, long nights can get longer.

On Demo D-Day, Ali's in bed by 1:30 am and gets up at 5:30 – the show starts at 8.

White as a sheet, he joins Duke and Casper, who look significantly better. They're carrying boxes with laptops, a projector and a mountain of cables. The guards at the door eye them even more suspiciously than usual and inspect everything twice for security purposes.

They're nervous. The devil's in the detail. Will the Wi-Fi work? Will the projector do what it's meant to?

Whether true or not, the bunqers feel like it's vital for their demo to be convincing, as DNB won't clear their schedule again. One hiccup and it'll all be over.

Sergey has outdone himself by managing to code OCR (Optical Character Recognition) into the demo. It can identify characters from a picture. Robbert, a TransIP legend, helped him do it.

Ali attributes the bulk of TransIP's success to his talented colleagues. When in need, he calls on them, as he did when the OCR wouldn't stabilize.

It works now: take a picture of your passport, and the fields required to register with bunq fill themselves in. If the Wi-Fi's working, that is. And today of all days, DNB's Wi-Fi is not.

The attendees' overfilled schedules don't allow for overrunning. Quickly, Ali improvises, and uses a collection of mobile phones to create a hotspot that allows them to show their demo anyway.

Working up to the highlight, the OCR demonstration, Ali's hands tremble as he reaches for his iPhone and passport. If the image shakes too much, OCR won't recognize the letters. So he buys a few seconds by talking about it while trying to stabilize his hand. Still shaking and with bated breath, he holds the passport in front of the camera... and... it works!

The bunqers are incredibly proud and relieved, but the DNBers seem unimpressed. They mainly bang on about the process of accepting clients. At bunq, you can open an account within a few minutes, using the app. This is unprecedented. How do you stop a system with such a low threshold from being abused and used for money laundering practices and the funding of terrorism? Although these questions have all been answered in writing — more than once — they are answered yet again in person.

'We launch on December 12, 2014.' Duke ends the meeting with Oscar-worthy certainty.

The next day, Ali visits DNB a third time. He realizes that this really is D-Day: the day of the decision. It's all about the thumb-thick corporate governance file and other final necessities for the permit.

Ali sits with his back to the wall. He suspects it was purposefully planned that way. Facing him is the head of payment traffic - an IT expert, the head of reviews and the head of bank supervision. Ali finds them to be direct, sharp-witted and authentic - which he likes.

The conversation doesn't adhere to a strict protocol and it contains real questions. The second one that pops up is:

'Assuming bunq is successful, what effect would that have on existing banks?'

Ali's pleasantly taken off-guard. So far every what-if question has been about the exit strategy: what if bunq fails?

He outlines a scenario he considers most realistic. New clients are likely to want to use bunq as a second account, like a WhatsApp for payments. If bunq really becomes a successful, established brand, they may eventually move their salaries to their bunq accounts.

The scenario is a lot more modest than in the early days of Project Clear. Back then, they really saw themselves as a competitor to the banks. They were the anti-bank, free of the diseases of the banking world. Every existing bank was a potential enemy. Since then, they've gained the confidence and introspection to know that bunq can exist alongside other banks, not necessarily instead of them.

Another one of those questions: 'We're used to people who want to make money. Your business plan doesn't mention a Return on Investment anywhere. What's in it for you?'

The easiest question so far for Ali — since this is what truly drives him. He answers: 'we want to bring change and shape the future. Creating history, as they say at my university, TU Delft. Earning some money in the process is a logical consequence.'

'In that case, we have a problem,' the head of supervision of banks responds. 'We're used to dealing with board members who work based on ROI. That makes them predictable since we can predict ROI's. You, however...'

Every subsequent question slips further in between the

chinks in Ali's armor. His weaknesses are mapped out and then pierced with sharp remarks.

'You're going to do something with iOS. I don't believe in that,' says the head of payment traffic. 'I have a Windows phone. How do I sign up?'

'You don't. We won't cover every platform,' Ali answers.

'So you don't listen to your clients?'

'Of course we do. But as Henry Ford said: If I'd asked people what they wanted, they'd have said "faster horses". We invent our own ideas and strategies, rather than create what others might want. We focus on who we want to be. But we strongly believe in the client's freedom of choice. They can stick with their old bank, or, if they want fun and change, they can join us. There's not one standard bicycle shop to suit everyone either, is there?

By the end of an exhausting hour-and-a-half, Ali has a question too: 'How did I do? I understand that I'm not your typical CEO...'

'That's right. You'll be hearing from us.'

Fifteen minutes later, he's faced with a second battle. The head of the admission-team. He's found an inconsistency in the numbers in one of the documents. The division of sums in the business plan differs from that in a later document. Can Ali expand on the ICAAP?

ICAAP is the Internal Capital Adequacy Assessment Process. It's a document that describes how much capital you need, where this capital comes from and how you make sure it's sufficient to cover the risks.

'There's no discrepancy between the methods of calculation,' Ali explains. The spotted difference boils down to the nine months bunq spent waiting for an appointment with DNB.

The Catch-22 is also discussed. Ali and Duke have tried to explain the paradox to their case manager on several occasions. They've even offered possible solutions, like: provide a conditional license with certain prerequisites, so that bunq can move on and finally access much needed documentation.

The head of admissions tells them that the IT-requirements will not create a hold-up. It has been decided to go for a conditional license, and the IT-requirements will be one of the preconditions in that agreement.

It's a huge weight off of Ali's shoulders.

Finally, but not unexpectedly, his own position at bunq turns out to be a sensitive and yet-to-be-resolved issue.

DNB wants to avoid a new DSB at all cost. The collapse of that bank is still a huge thorn in the supervisor's side. It seems to Ali that this attitude is based on emotion rather than rationality, and more on personal rather than professional reasons. After all, banks with other forms of shareholder structures went bankrupt too. The crash of ABN Amro and SNS for example. Or the emergency financing of ING. Both cost society much more than DSB did. The only difference is that in the case of DSB, it was much easier to point a finger towards the director/main shareholder.

And so returns the repeated what-if question: what if bunq fails?

DNB demands a guarantee in hard cash. Ali or TransIP have to hand over a non-refundable deposit. He literally has to distance himself from all money that is currently in bunq and any money yet to be contributed. That's a lot. But it's certainly not more than he was willing to put in from the start: every dime he owns.

The down payment turns out to be a lot higher than originally thought. The beer coaster calculations amounted to no more than five to six million. Financing would, as planned, go through TransIP. DNB, however, believes their activities carry more risk, and therefore wants a much larger buffer. The legally required five million is just their starting point. After adding it all together — including the loss of time and amount of work — results in a staggering seventeen million euros.

And they don't have that kind of money.

A Gap of Millions

The rainy summer of 2014 doesn't dampen the excitement at bunq. A successful demo, good reviews, a decent relationship with DNB, ... they're convinced they'll get their permit.

Duke shares the optimism, except for one thing: the positive developments aren't doing much to bring in the big clients. Having them on board would really help to make bunq a relevant player. Especially now.

bunq's strategy comes straight out of the TransIP playbook: offer loads and ask little in return. It's what made TransIP great and it revolutionized the world of web hosting. Once they have their banking license, bunq is free to determine its own rates. Provided bunq grows big enough. And to become big, they need big partners.

For the past month bunq has had an actual Support Team in place in charge of customer support. Its first member is Hans Peter: laid back, clever and funny, he's a typical defensive midfielder in a team of friends. 'HP', as his friends call him, studied business administration and specialized in strategy & organization. He takes the train from Utrecht, and at the age of 27, he's one of the older bunqers. Because their users — the personal account holders — are imaginary for the foreseeable future, so is the Support Team. And so HP joins business development: where in the market will we find our clients, and why?

He's supported by Diederick, Stijn aka 'Stini', and Anne.

Diederick is a blond, left-handed Viking, chilled out

with a quiet tendency to take the lead. He studied industrial management & engineering in Groningen.

Stini, a proper Rotterdammer (born & raised in Rotterdam), worked at Heineken. His speech is filled with raw remarks, and every now and then he speaks of 'chickies' who 'ain't scared', to suggest a woman's romantic interest.

Anne was a wedding planner at the Amstel Hotel. She's always cheerful and can be a little blunt in an endearing sort of way. She's also really good at looking angry, though it's nearly always feigned anger. She's somewhat of a national celebrity, since she took part in a television game show. HP hooked her up with a job at bunq.

The team, led by Duke, is responsible for convincing companies to offer bunq payments alongside cards and the leading Dutch online payment system iDEAL.

They hit the road, armed with copies of the non-disclosure agreement. Small companies are charmed by that. The agreement implies something exclusive and promising. At larger firms who have their own legal departments, it mostly slows things down.

Their pitch goes along the lines of: 'Using bunq doesn't just save time and effort, it saves money, too, as there's no hardware required'. It's just words. Just like at DNB, a demo is more convincing.

Duke gives a full-scale presentation at an educational institution in Amsterdam, but it's only once he shows them the demo that it takes them three minutes to decide. Their timing is also impeccable: the chip payment system is going out of commission and people are looking for something new.

Because everything at bunq is intertwined, the separate

teams grow closer and closer together. Duke and Ali's tasks begin to overlap. Their interdependence increases and with that, the friction.

Ali is worried about their lack of progress. Time is running out and he feels responsible for everything – including acquiring big clients, which is technically Duke's responsibility.

Despite Duke's optimism, and despite all the positive reactions: the big clients just aren't there. Duke blames it on the stalemate: how to get clients through the door when you don't have a working product and can't even say with certainty when there will be one? Ali calls it a lame excuse. In turn, Ali's impatience and interference make Duke's blood boil.

After a meeting with the Supervisory Board, when Ali and the others are no longer in the room, Duke can't restrain himself and says: 'in the end it's Ali who is responsible for our commercial success, of course'. And isn't it Ali who keeps throwing out the code and starting over with IT?

Although Ali's continuous fatigue refuses to fade, his mind is functioning a little better. He also has more room to think now that he's dealt with all the interrogations, reviews, demos and searches for new board members.

This finally allows him to delve deeper into the technical details of the payments systems. They MacGyver their way around their lack of permit to scavenge all the information they need. Slowly but surely it flows in by drips and drabs.

Because of Ali's overview of nearly everything, he's able to see and anticipate imperfections in the process.

The coders know that they have to lay a foundation that is as solid as possible, so that they can build on it for many years to come. Menno, one of the new programmers, even thinks that the current code is the best he's ever laid eyes on. But they also realize that they might not be building on the most solid of foundations. They are still forced to base everything on abstractions, options and speculations. They have a long way to go.

It's Friday the 29th of August. Ali sits down with Robert-Jan ('RJ'), a coder and member of the exclusive 0-club since January: the small group of bunqers that made 0 mistakes on the logical reasoning test that forms part of the job application process. After fifteen minutes, Ali's seen enough: 'Refactor it,' he orders. He means: restructure the entire code.

It's a harsh conclusion – yet again. The 'best ever' code just isn't good enough. Again. It's too complicated, too contradictory. And no, there's no point continuing work with this as a foundation. Because, yes, the code functions, but that doesn't necessarily benefit the structure as a whole, and it might even end up undermining it.

'If you lay the groundwork for a three-story building, and then realize it's going to be ten stories, you have to start again,' he explains to an astounded RJ. Besides, now that they keep getting a slow trickle of technical details, they can finally start for real. And properly this time.

RJ defends the code and the discussion grows into an argument. Petros, too, struggles to hide his emotions. To be fair, it's the fourth time Ali makes him throw out all of his blood, sweat and tears.

But Ali's decision has been made. He notifies the Supervisory Board of this one final rewrite.

A day after the code is shot down, RJ goes on vacation. He packs his suitcase with tears in his bloodshot eyes. The timing could not have been worse.

Ali's crushed the code. And there's not much sight of getting that seventeen million euro deposit together either.

For a sum of that size, they'll need a loan. The only issue is that bunq needs to keep their activities secret, as they're developing to compete with existing banks. This makes it nearly impossible to get a loan on their own and the original plan to get a loan through TransIP was based on only a third of the now required amount.

Now that financing has become an issue, TransIP is doing its rounds of the banks, just in case. 'What's the financing for', they ask? 'Ali's new initiative,' is the answer. The exact destination of the funds is irrelevant, as long as you get it back, right?

After a primary exploration, the three large Dutch banks remain – ABN Amro, ING and Rabobank. The latter turns up at TransIP with no fewer than two directors for a chat with Ali. But the meeting is interrupted: there's a technical fault due to a failing hard drive containing crucial information, and Ali is asked to help fix it. He wants to get through the conversation as quickly as possible and he enters the room with his heels dug in.

'I was very impressed with ING Alkmaar, they were really constructive. But then they split up the team and we got other people who put themselves first. I hate it when banks put themselves ahead of the client. I certainly hope Rabobank doesn't fall into that category.'

He'll never find out. Upset by the tone of the conversation, Rabobank pulls out.

TransIP has had great ties with both ING and ABN Amro for years, but in Spreadsheet Land, well-presented numbers outweigh relationships. They need someone to sort that out. Luckily Duke and Ali know just the guy, and they have him in-house.

A second Peter, a Dutch one this time, has joined the start-up as an international business developer. He has a history at ING Alkmaar, which is where Ali met him. He's part of the team that Ali described to Rabobank. Peter and Ali worked together on the creation of The Datacenter Group. Some years ago a huge building was bought and revamped to house IT equipment for large organizations.

Ali calls his contact at ABN Amro, while Peter enters the numbers into a format that bankers like. Both ABN and ING make an offer. Eventually, the latter 'wins'.

Through a capital contribution from TransIP, the money ends up with bunq. 14.5 million euros are parked at DNB as a deposit. In order to reach the required 16.7 million, Ali empties his own pockets. It amounts to all of the profit TransIP has saved up over the years. It's a non-refundable deposit, so it's the last he'll see of it.

bunq is suddenly the only 'bank' in the world with more capital of its own than that of their clients' bank accounts. It's the epitome of full reserve banking, like they once thought they could be by storing their money at DNB.

The IT-driven service provider that doesn't want to be a bank – the new rebel in town challenging the existing banks – get's to see the light of day, thanks to... a bank.

The Eagle

6:39 pm on a Wednesday, September 3, 2014, Pieter receives an email headed: 'State of affairs concerning banking license application'. DNB reports their 'intention' of offering bunq a banking license, 'under certain conditions'. And that, once the conditions have been met, bunq may begin its banking activities.

He immediately forwards the message to Duke and Ali and calls them straight after.

Ali happens to be visiting Docters van Leeuwen at that exact moment. The weakened guard dog is at home, tortured and exhausted. It makes the moment even more beautiful as he shares his ecstasy with the man who was there right from the start. He was the first to take the risk of linking his name to the venture. Docters van Leeuwen himself is euphoric too – pleased that the time has finally come.

Shortly after he hangs up the phone, Pieter suddenly gets a stabbing pain in his stomach, as though the release of tension has manifested itself physically. A few hours later, he can't take it anymore and goes to the out-of-hours GP service. No doctor can determine what's wrong. They fear an infection or, worse, a tumor. Despite the potentially gruesome underlying cause, Pieter's main concern is that he won't be at bunq when the seal of approval actually arrives.

The following day Ali visits him in hospital. In bed lies a broken man, doped up on morphine but still in pain.

Next to him is his daughter, cheerful and caring, just like her father.

Pieter's stay in hospital passes without any further notification from DNB. He's initially relieved, because both the pain in his stomach and his fear of missing the moment disappear. During the weekend, his mood changes back to worry. Why is there still no word from DNB this time?

In the absence of their CFRO, Duke has taken to doing what Pieter did so many times: make phone calls to DNB. Not once, not twice, but constantly.

When he finally manages to get ahold of someone in the know, the reason for the silence turns out to be rather silly. Their contact, the one who's supposed to write the letter, is simply still on vacation.

At the end of the following week, Pieter returns home. An old wound turned out to have healed up wrong: scar tissue fused to healthy tissue and closed off his small intestine. A minor surgery fixed the problem.

Resting at home, he receives a phone call: a letter is underway, both as a hard copy and digitally. And indeed on that Tuesday, September 16, 2014, it arrives: the email. Pieter forwards it to Duke and Ali at the speed of light. He changes the subject header to: 'The eagle has landed.'

In words that are not triumphant, but meaningful, DNB reports that it is granting bunq a permit for the execution of banking services. The conditions include the functioning of the IT and a series of security matters. History in the making! For the first time in all these years, Ali allows himself and the others an afternoon off.

The musical beats at Orly Square thump even louder than

usual. Bags of chips are sprawled across the table. The bunqers grab beers from fridges and crates. A few of them run to the kiosk at the station to buy the thickest cigar available: 'We're bankers and we'd better believe it!'

The next morning, a large box is delivered. In it they find white T-shirts with bunq-green ties with the words 'Official Banker Wankers' printed across them. A joke from a few of the guys over at TransIP.

On Thursday, when Pieter's fit enough, the gang heads out to Pacific Parc, a rock 'n roll bar and dance café nearby. Although relieved and joyful, they still need to keep a lid on their plans as much as possible. bunq is still nowhere near ready to go live and Duke and Ali are still paranoid when it comes to the established banks. They've asked DNB to keep this historic moment as quiet as possible. But then the law gets in the way.

Article 1:107 of the Law pertains to financial supervision and outlines the 'public banking register'. It publicizes which banks may, as of which time, undertake which actions. All certified banks (and other financial ventures) are listed here. Any alteration must be published within one working day.

The register offers a 'six-week term of objection'. It feels just as old-fashioned as the 'notice of marriage', allowing third parties to object to a wedding. Whatever objection an existing bank might have, the consequence is delay. And Public means that the register is publicly announced. *Het Financieele Dagblad*, among others, subscribes to this service. They may not find it worthy of publication in the editorial office, or at the most they might mention it briefly in one column or another. But: publicity is publicity. With

ING as their neighbor, bunq prefers to keep all windows shut.

Because absolute secrecy seems to have become impossible, Ali phones Paul van Liempt from his car to finally lift a tip of the veil with regard to 'Project X', as he promised he would. Van Liempt calls it 'mega news', but he's happy to keep quiet until bunq's ready.

For months, bunq worked in a continuous climate of uncertainty. The increasingly hopeful expectations mounted to a static charge in the final weeks with sparks of nervous excitement. It all suddenly feels very real. The tension discharges with a bang. A hard and unprecedented clash ensues.

The reason is as stupid as it is futile. Now that, thanks to the banking register, bunq might be Googled, they need a website. To accompany their online 'coming out', Ali wants to add a subtitle: 'free from the established elite'. Pieter, still in bed, disagrees wholeheartedly. If you're paranoid about what existing banks might do, why give a cause for confrontation? It's exactly the anti-bank attitude that agitated Docters van Leeuwen from the start. It's asking for trouble.

Ali promises to have another look at the text. He feels these five words perfectly capture what they're fighting against. Also, it's not an isolated matter. The phrase fits the concept of the rest of the website and the email they've created. Altering the words means having to alter the whole thing altogether.

A day of thinking doesn't result in a satisfactory alternative. He asks another Pieter, nicknamed 'The Slooth' to call Pieter van der Harst. The first Pieter, whose photography adorned the walls of their very first office, has since joined Djoeri in overseeing online matters.

Both Pieters sincerely attempt to help each other, but they get confused. From that moment on, whenever Ali suggests something to one Pieter, the other Pieter's opinion is also asked for. And Ali is well aware that opinions are killers in marketing. It's like soccer: everyone thinks they understand it simply because they have an opinion about it. At some point the confused communication even causes unclarity as to which language they will be communicating in: English or Dutch?

'Ask me or ask Pieter, but don't ask both of us, or we'll never get anywhere,' Ali snarls at Djoeri, who feels like he and The Slooth have been placed in an impossible position.

A slightly garbled version of this sentence makes its way to Pieter van der Harst. The friendliest man alive explodes. It all centers around that one line: 'free from the established elite'. Pieter is against it and Duke unexpectedly changes his mind from yay to nay.

Ali refuses to go on like this and announces that he's going to take a vacation. His head hurts, he's exhausted, he cannot take another step and it shows. The coders, not exactly talkative by nature, hide behind their screens.

At night, when things calm down, Djoeri drops by Ali's desk. They've known each other for a long time, and they know each other well. Ali explains his frustration: 'Changing things, fine. But I can't live with a half-baked website as our first public expression.'

'But you're not going to let it fall apart now, are you?' Djoeri reprimands him.

'No, But It Has To Be Good,' Ali spells out, slightly less hotheaded. 'Anything less is unacceptable.'

Ali calls Pieter: 'I'm in charge of marketing. I'll take your opinion into consideration, but I need space to work. You'll see what's been decided on Monday.'

In that case I quit, thinks Pieter. But he doesn't say what he's thinking. That Monday, the website goes live with a new message.

> Independent
> The bank with a clean slate

A milestone email goes out to the Inner Circle. The message also serves as a friendly reminder of the non-disclosure agreement:

> It's official. bunq is the first Dutch greenfield bank of the century (and in decades, for that matter) to independently obtain a banking permit. The go-ahead was given on September 17. A lot of details remain unknown to the public. Don't spoil the fun and please keep honoring your NDA!

Pieter's completely happy with it. They make up and Ali readily admits that Pieter's argument led to a better result, and that's all that counts. Always.

They blame their clash on the extreme tension that's built up over this period as well as the physical distance. And the other one's stubbornness. Because, hey, that's just what the other is like...

Either way, their paranoid attitude towards other banks appears exaggerated if not unfounded. Even after publication in the banking register, no one pays any notice to bunq. One month later, on October 30, 2014, during a 'European Retail Banking Conference', Ralph Hamers, CEO of the ING Group, makes the following statement:

> 'There is much talk of tech companies wanting to become banks. That is not what I see. Do not forget that the banking industry is a highly regulated one. (...) Tech companies are not used to this. Their natural environment is much less regulated. Therefore, I think technology companies do not even want to become banks!'

Goodbye

bunq's reception is directly to the left of the entrance. A ceramic head with a diameter of nearly one meter is carefully placed onto a column by two art handlers. A little man, also ceramic, appears to have climbed on top of the large head. A subtle inscription reads: *use your brain*. On the pillar also lies an album filled with poems by Belgian artist Lebuïn D'Haese.

Sometimes a branch, a twig
is moved by the wind
sometimes by a bird, a sparrow, promptly
the tough branch bends
The larger the tree
the greater the strength
to offer resistance
against storms, against vultures

At the end of the long, bright corridor is the canteen, the main living space. This is where they have lunch, hold presentations and parties, all announced by a loud bang of the gong. It's also where people sit when the offices are full, which is happening more and more often.

There's an open kitchen overlooking eight long scaffold-board tables, two massive fridges (one of which is purely for beer), a ping-pong table, a hammock and a 12-seater sofa. The music playlist is continuous, either 'party' or 'classic rock'.

The full height windows, the painted floor and the white ceiling make for a bright and airy feel. The windows offer a bird's-eye view of the train and metro traffic of Amsterdam Sloterdijk Station on one side, and railway lines, tarmac roads, high rise buildings and the fields beyond on the other. Even though none of the windows open, the air in the entire space feels fresh.

On the left side of the corridor, just before the canteen, four pallets are attached to the wall with large metal hooks. They serve as a pin board and are covered in photographs, emails and newspaper articles.

'It is now possible to transfer money via Facebook or phone'

'Railway chief: paying by transport card is old fashioned.'

'Aegon bank still no success.'

A frayed orange poster says: 'Hurray! The ING App's 3rd birthday'. Someone's written 'bunq' over the top of 'ING' and '1' over '3'.

There are more developments in the field of electronic payment than the pallets can take. Vodafone and Visa are launching their Smartpass. You can deposit cash onto the card: it doubles up as a prepaid credit card and it's free to use for the first year. It's the initiative Dutch banks tried to stay ahead of with their test in Leiden.

Apple signs an agreement with MasterCard, American Express and Visa for an iPhone 6 payment system: Apple-Pay. An NFC chip turns your phone into a wallet. As with the launch of Yosemite, riddled with bugs, or the Apple Watch with all of its issues, Apple fans react less enthusiastically than when Steve Jobs was still alive: *NFC is sooo 2002...*

BPCE, a large French bank, has hooked up with Twitter to enable people to tweet money back and forth. They've come up with a payment app: S-money. Twitter has been arguing with Facebook for some time as to who will beat the other to an attractive payment service. Facebook is starting a collaboration to enable the transfer of money to Facebook friends.

bunq might be well ahead of Apple and its NFC chip in regards to innovation — at least in terms of payment technology and coding — but payment via Twitter or Facebook gets dangerously close to what bunq's doing. That makes them nervous.

Duke's brave announcement in July of a launch on December 12, 2014, turns out to have been a little optimistic now that all of the information is accessible. Although the permit is now conditionally theirs, a functioning app is as far out of reach as it ever was. Compared to these swift developments, bunq is suddenly lagging behind.

After scrapping the code nearly three months ago, Petros took RJ's place for two weeks during the latter's vacation. It was a dramatic shift, filled with frustration. He and Ali constantly argued over progress, leading to several screaming matches a day. When RJ returned after two weeks there was barely any progress to speak of. Loads of code had been removed, but barely any had been added.

Ali renamed one of the offices to 'The PAIN ROOM. Where you learn to type'. It's a place for bunqers to sit and get their code reviewed by Ali. Line by line. Just as long until something good comes out.

He and RJ get seriously stuck in at the back-end. They

spend day and night glued to a king-size screen full of endless lines of code. The other coders type on as well. Seven days a week, fourteen to sixteen hours a day. They vow to be ready to start a pilot in December. A small group of testers will try out the app and note down any bugs so that the coders can improve on it. That should allow them to launch bunq sometime in the first quarter of 2015.

After his brief elation following receipt of the permit, Ali is soon back to feeling like he's fighting a war of attrition. The license should have been the go ahead for bunq to enter the outside world, but it turns out to be nothing but the start of a new phase, in which nearly everything is waiting on what he and the IT team are doing. And they're not doing well enough. Time and time again he's unsatisfied with the results: 'Start again!'

They need to do more – and fast. The iOS app is shaky as hell, so he flies in Andreas, one of TransIP's star talents. The DevOps department – a combination of developer and system operator – is a mess. DevOps develops software and makes sure the servers and the network function properly. TransIP has the strongest DevOps department of the Netherlands and two of their best professionals are Reinier and Johan. Both of them join the ranks.

The complex and exhausting coding leads to a quick and continuous selection process. Only the best of the best stay standing. Their qualities complement and enhance one another.

Newbie 'Sven', for example, just young enough for bunq at 26, has a phenomenal insight into abstractions. Wessel, 24, was snatched fresh out of Delft Technical University in 2014. He has a natural feel for order and complex structures. Patrick is even newer and younger. He's 22, and doesn't just understand user interaction, he has a real affinity for it. He looks a bit like Ed Sheeran. Ali, who's in his early thirties, is an old man to them. The team now counts sixteen altogether.

Despite their hard work, it soon turns out that a pilot in December is impossible. A new estimate puts it six months away. It's a period they can't shorten. It's going to be a while before the coders receive the data they need to connect to the card payment programs.

Ali proceeds to lay claim to the largest office and sticks a sheet of A4 to the door: 'PRO ROOM'. Only true pros are allowed in. Ali wields his scepter ruthlessly, symbolized by a large black whip swinging from the wall of the Pro Room.

During their forward sprint, the coders go through kilograms of 'code candy' each day: dishes full of sweets to fuel the fire. At night, their strip-lit discussions are no longer heated, but driven.

With the foundation being laid afresh, it's going to be a long time before anyone gets to see any of the fruits of their labor. With nothing to go on, more and more bunqers wonder what's going on in Ali's damaged brain.

'Das wichtigste steht nicht in den Noten', composer Gustav Mahler once said. 'The most important part is not written in the notes'. In coding, it really is the notes that matter, and a single incorrect one can screw up the entire concert. Why did Ali figure that out so late, each time, causing so much delay? Of course it's a matter of trial and error. But another valid answer: his mind.

Ali receives the results of an examination performed by two neurological teams. One in Austria and one in the Netherlands. He had a 4.5 centimeter tear in his skull and a subdural hematoma: a blood clot in between two membranes of the brain. He should have been admitted to hospital straight after his fall to drain excess fluid and lower pressure in the brain. But because he wasn't, he's now irreversibly brain damaged. 'Damaged brain cells won't regenerate, what you are now is what you're going to be,' one of the doctors explains to him over the phone.

His creativity is impaired, his thoughts are slower, his concentration is gone and he has trouble controlling the left side of his body. The medical expectation is that he will never be able to view the world as sharply as he did before. A large number of his original capacities will recover slowly, but not all of them.

Ali experiences it as a huge loss and is intensely saddened. How much further along would we be, he curses to himself, if I hadn't fallen?

December 5, a Dutch national holiday, which should be a festive evening full of jokes and presents, the mood in the office is subdued. Ali is the most subdued of all, but he doesn't show it.

There are seven members in the Suicide Club. Amongst them are two pillars of strength: Jordi and Sergey.

Lawyer Jordi has always felt like the odd one out. He was the only one who continued to follow a corporate dress code, surrounded by hoodies and techno music. He's never managed to get used to the street fighter mentality and highly informal organizational structures. In hindsight, the banking license was a massive intellectual challenge. But now there's nothing more for him at bunq — or so he feels. A full team of specialists takes his place. Dominik and two newcomers: Daan ('Jaws') and Quirijn.

Sergey wants to return to his passion of all that is new. He's found things at bunq that he hasn't found anywhere else, like the all-consuming 'stop talking — start typing'. The simple principle of 'be practical and use your brain' wasn't just a slogan here, it was actually how they worked. But bunq's changed. Everything's become more serious. There's no more time to try things out, everything has to be fast and reliable. DNB demands it, the timeline demands it and so does the technology. They have to get their systems in order and get on with the coding. Sergey's more of a creator — not someone who produces quickly and with great consideration. He's just not the best man for the job during this current phase, and he knows it. So he leaves. With no hard feelings, but with regret. However frustrated he was with Ali's repeated destruction of the code, he's been inspired by his courage not to avoid confrontation, and thereby arrive at the unattainable.

Another professional relationship is under even greater pressure. Business development isn't going the way Ali wants it to. If it were his team, he would have intervened long before. But because it's Duke's, he's more cautious. Arguing that the two disciplines are increasingly intertwined, and will be even more so in the future, Ali suggests setting up a joint weekly meeting for the marketing and business development teams.

The introduction goes smoothly. In the second or third week however, things go south. David, who answers directly to Duke, schedules the meeting on a day that Duke is absent. It rubs Duke the wrong way.

Duke and Ali's relationship has been shifting for some time. In the beginning, there was an equal input of knowledge and contacts, as well as clear complementary competencies. Two years later, the situation and the relationships have changed.

Instead of the initial five, including Duke's brother, his friends and his intern, thirty people now work at bunq, all of whom are twenty years younger than him. Also, Duke feels held back in his work. The pressure on him has been rising due to the lack of commercial success. But how can he draw large clients without a decent product to show?

He has to vent his frustration. He decides to 'escalate up'.

Duke speaks to his fellow member of the Board of Directors, Pieter, telling him that Ali is undermining him. Subsequently, he calls one of the members of the Supervisory Board for advice. He chooses to skip a conversation with Ali on this occasion.

Ali hears about it through the grapevine. He finds Duke's response 'corporate': a natural stress response has caused Duke to return to familiar patterns and old behavior, in line with previous professional experiences, which are, therefore, political. Ali, on the other hand, would be more likely to apply a direct approach and street fighter tactics.

Their conflict has now also become a matter for the Supervisory Board.

Duke feels that bunq is entering into a new phase and should adapt its structure accordingly. If they added a layer of management beneath him and Ali, it would give them time to work on strategy, instead of focusing on day-today issues. Ali, who is just as likely to fall back into old, familiar practices, is currently interfering with everything. To Ali, unity is the company's main strength. Compartmentalizing or 'layering' would lead to inefficiency.

In the meantime, his efforts have already resulted in an organic and undeniable middle layer. bunq is growing at the speed of light, and the teams are growing with it. Some employees stand out in terms of leadership, others shine when it comes to content and specialistic knowledge. It isn't a hierarchy that dictates their place, but the organization's ability to self-manage. No one calls him or herself 'manager'. That's a tainted term amongst young bunqers, as it implies an artificial structure. Since when is knowledge subordinate to organizational talent?

Duke fails to find backing for his proposal.

HOPE

Too Close for Comfort

It's 5 am on January 7, 2015, and 25-year-old marketer Marc is still working... It's his first time working until this late, but he suspects it won't be his last. With the impersonal glow of two fluorescent lights, he's been entering the transaction costs and fees of all Dutch banks into an Excel document. It's painstaking work.

The 24-hour economy of a start-up has little consideration for diurnal rhythms. 5 am is not an unusual time to close your laptop at bunq. Because of this, one of the offices has been set up as a bedroom. A cabinet separates paper, folders, screens and phones in storage from a narrow single bed by the window.

Just as Marc is about to lie down, fully dressed, he remembers he hasn't locked his bike. Now, Amsterdam's nowhere near the worst city in the Netherlands when it comes to bike theft (measured by municipality and per 1,000 inhabitants, that's Groningen, followed by one of the Wadden Islands), but still. Amsterdam may not even be in the top 10, but the sense of security is different from that on an island. And so, with a few hours to go until sunrise, Marc takes the elevator down, only to find the front doors ajar.

Their building at Orly Square has a glass entrance with two sliding doors. From the outside, they open if you press the right code. From the inside, one only needs to activate the motion sensor. Usually, they're shut tight. Now, there's a gap wide enough to let in a person sideways.

There are two vans from a security company parked thirty meters up the road, at Sloterdijk Station. Marc walks over. The gentlemen can't help him: they only guard the train station, not the neighboring buildings. They inform him however that someone just tried to break into the kiosk.

Marc rushes back and calls Securitas, the company in charge of their building's security. They ask for 'his code', to enable them to take action. Marc calls 'Vincent', aka 'the Dominator', whose duties include being in charge of security. Dominik, as he's actually called, doesn't have the code. He'll have to call 1-1-2, the Dutch emergency number.

Within a few minutes, a police car arrives. Two officers enter the building with Marc and call in a second car to stop the burglars in case they try to flee.

Marc guides the officers through the building. They check every door. They're all closed on the ground floor as well as on the first. They continue until they reach the fourth floor. bunq's door bounces open and they enter carefully. Marc closes the door and they move up a floor.

In the corner of the fifth floor they find a homeless guy. His trousers are down and there is a pungent aroma of alcohol and urine. One of the officers wakes him. The homeless man seems to be speaking seven languages at once, none of which are coherent. Booze and schizophrenia have damaged his tongue and the part of his brain responsible for speech.

The officers drag the man to his feet and take him away. During the five-floor elevator ride down, the man stares accusingly at Marc in the lift mirror. Once they're outside, the man is free to go. The building's door was shoved open without causing damage. It doesn't qualify as breaking and entering but merely an unauthorized entry.

Homeless people and miscreants will tell you that safety and ease of access are contradictory terms. A steel shutter will keep people out better than a sliding glass door, but it won't make for customer friendly access. If your building looks like a bunker, it's hard to sell an image of transparency.

The same goes for payment systems. The more you board a system up, the safer it is, but the more difficult to access. You have to fill in a code, use an 'e.dentifier', and who knows how many security gateways.

At bunq, a fierce battle is being fought between safety and ease of access. bunq must be super-safe, or they'll lose their provisional license. It will have to be dragged through the Cobit wringer: Control Objectives for Information and Related Technology, a corporate governance model for IT. At the same time, user friendly access is vital to bunq. The whole point is to be a purely mobile service provider. No one will spend money on a system that scares them off with security measures or appears unsympathetic.

bunq wants bulletproof glass: invisible and protective, user friendly and safe. To create a new account, a photo of your ID will suffice. You fill in a few personal preferences and upload a profile picture. No need for paper, envelopes, numbers or waiting times. The record for the quickest registration is 4 minutes and 34 seconds, but they want to get it even quicker.

During onboarding, the bunq-term for registration, several immediate safety checks take place based on the user's documents and social security number. The back-end, the part of the programming the user can't see, is filled with checks and measures to counter any attempted violations.

Meanwhile, Duke's position has become very difficult. His usually sparkling eyes are now dull. The conditional banking permit makes it a lot easier for parties to sign the NDA, but there are still no game changing partnerships. The large companies are in no hurry. Besides, their clients have the power to make or break bunq's relevance in the market. They use that as a form of negotiation.

Andrew sees several of his closest associates keeping bunq at arm's length, although they'd previously committed. He expresses his annoyance at the excessive time gap between the initial introduction and the launch, which is still not even in sight.

Suddenly, and without consultation, Duke dissolves his business development team in the beginning of March 2015. According to him the business and marketing teams now effectively operate under Ali anyway. David, who works directly with Duke, feels stuck in the middle.

Ali says the sudden dissolving of the business team doesn't serve any logical goal. He thinks it's an irrational, emotional decision. He sees no point in confronting Duke with the matter; a discussion based on emotions is bound to fail anyways...

He complains to Pieter: 'This is never-ending'.

The CFRO doesn't ask him what he means. The constant postponing of the pilot? The new Catch-22? The frictions between him and Duke? Everything is so entangled.

Ten days later, nearly all of bunq departs for a team-building trip in the Ardennes. The destination is a former hotel in Stoumont, near Liège. The town is by the Lienne, an idyllic little river that meanders in between eroded mountains covered in pine trees. The straightest line in sight is the railway track, on which two trains meet once a day.

Pieter's trip to the Ardennes is preceded by an intercontinental tour. His brother has nearly finished a project in Australia, and Pieter hasn't had a chance to visit him in the four years that his brother has lived there. He wanted to go for at least three weeks to make it worth the long flight. But three weeks off turned out to be impossible during his time at RBS and bunq. Now that his brother's about to leave, all he can manage is a one-week visit.

Back from Down Under after a 24-hour flight, Pieter drives straight to bunq in the morning. Just after 3 pm, he sets off again with jet lag and a car full of coders. At 6:30 pm they finally roll past a sign that reads 'Stoumont'. Just in time for the pub quiz. The journey time to holiday time ratio is worse than his intercontinental flight, because at 9 pm that same evening, Pieter drives back to his family near Amsterdam.

The reason he wanted to at least show his face in Stoumont is because Duke's not there. The conflict between him and Ali has run too deep for that. The two of them staying there together would only increase the tension. It's so very different from their last retreat after the license application, when everything was still fine.

In the meantime a compromise has been struck to Duke's disadvantage. Duke only gets to focus on large potential clients and international affairs, and he's halved his working week. Ali gets business development, Pieter gets the legal part.

The bunqers approach the pub quiz in Stoumont like a cup final. Focused and with gritted teeth, they throw themselves at the questions. Scoring is the number one priority. A relaxed walk in the woods the next day turns into a muddy race. New goal: be first to cross the finish line.

A zealous and decisive urge to perform is a dominant trait among bunqers. The fun is in the road to achievement. When there's nothing left to turn into a contest, the competition abates and everyone, regardless of their intense efforts to win, gets together and has a beer as one big family.

'The reward for our work?' a tipsy coder ponders on the banks of the Lienne, swelled by rainfall. 'It's the work itself and the long hours. The feeling that you matter. And the idea that the change we're creating might lead to a revolution...'

'We're getting really close now. We're nearly there,' says Ali as he and Mani, a new coder from Iceland, walk to Liège station to see off a colleague. 'We just need to go live. This is depleting everyone.'

A Magical Day

RJ is the first with the insights to see it. His head sinks slowly toward his keyboard during a sunrise in late March and he startles a neighboring coder from his concentration. With eyes closed he smiles: 'It's correct. It all adds up now. It has come together.'

Solid, comprehensible, sharp and elegant: the foundation has been laid. The DNA is pure, legible and functional. The work of Andreas, Reinier, Johan and all of the bunqers slot into place. The confrontations, discussions and frustrations in the Pain Room, the drudging hours in the Pro Room: it's all justified by the realization that the code is now unequivocally fit.

The results are finally visible to everyone. bunq can move on.

On April 13, 2015, the Supervisory Board is invited to Orly Square. Arthur Docters van Leeuwen is absent. His health has forced him to rely on regular phone calls and visits from Ali to maintain his personal involvement.

After months of being passed around the world of medicine, it turns out his problems aren't caused by his heart, but by too much pressure from brain fluid: Normal pressure hydrocephalus, in medical language. It has lead to unbearable headaches and symptoms that resemble a mild form of dementia. His concentration is diminished, he can't read, not even the papers.

With an operation reserved for a mere 350 people a year, surgeons have placed a tube in his ventricle. The tube connects to a little valve under his skin behind his ear. If the pressure in his ventricle rises, the valve opens up to siphon off the surplus brain fluid through another tube to his stomach, where it's broken down. Since then, he's been battling to regain his fitness.

'It is — has been — an unpleasant time,' Docters van Leeuwen confides in Ali, 'especially at the beginning. Very unpleasant. It depressed me at first, now it mostly disheartens me. As long as I can't return to a reasonable pattern of living, I don't see that changing.'

Ali understands all too well.

At 4:30 pm, half an hour behind schedule, the sound of the gong rings out across the fourth floor. Everyone knows what announcement Ali's about to make. At the expense of his and his coders' sleep, he's pushed forwards. Even for bunq standards, they've worked ridiculously hard. But finally... finally, it begins.

While Ali announces that it's a magical day and that bunq is now truly moving into the next phase, a little group of coders continues to type at a table in the corner. Without these final fixes, the app will jam and the pilot — the first of three that will form the final hurdles before the launch — won't start.

Pale and shaky, Ali acknowledges having pushed, scolded and asked the impossible of Team IT. And that they've proven the impossible to be possible: 'Although, even within bunq, few will understand just how impressive this is, I do. And let me tell you that you've truly amazed me!' Then Ali frankly admits that he's worn out and that HP will be responsible for explaining the procedure for the testing phase.

'During the first two weeks, eight testers will open accounts,' HP begins. 'Four will start on iOS and another four tomorrow on Android. After two weeks, we will draw conclusions. In small teams, we'll determine what works smoothly and what doesn't and report it. Then, once everything's tested and adapted, we take the system offline. We reset the database, remove all account data and transactions and do the whole thing allover again. Then, with a maximum of 1,500 people, we do an "invite-only beta test". Only our friends and family will take part. During this third phase, we basically repeat what we did before, but with more people and more time: five weeks. Then the whole thing shuts down again, we clean everything up and then... *lift-off!*'

Over the sound of popping bottles of beer and sparkling wine, HP asks for silence again: 'Each of you received one cent last week during the first real app transfer. Can everyone please return it, because we don't want a bonus culture here!'

The office next to the canteen is set up as a testing area: two sets of tables and chairs and a camera. Testers David and Dominik have different kinds of iPhones. Every model is tested as they all should be able to support their app.

HP opens his MacBook and chats to Andreas, Lucas and RJ, the back-end and iOS coders, who are sat at their own desk down the corridor. His role is to interpret the comments of the testers and pass them on. The coders then fix the problem and create a new version of the app. The results have to be perfect. 'We only get one chance to launch and we want to grab it fully,' says HP.

On his laptop, he can see everything that happens on the testers' iPhones. David and Dominik log on.

'Nearby payment...'

Press NearPay and the app searches for users in the surrounding area. David walks his iPhone to the canteen.

'Sixty meters, when it should be five. The distance measurement's wrong,' he says.

'Payment request... I gave the order, took a picture and sent it. Domi's not getting a push. Payment request is working...'

'Boring and unclear when a payment's been made. All status notifications — received payment, accepted payment, sent payment — all in one row. Confusing.'

bunq's not expecting many bugs in the iOS version. All public demos so far have been done on the iPhone. Most of what popped up those times was fixed in the run-up or aftermath. Sometimes even small bugs required them to start over, but at least they knew what did and didn't work.

The foundation is solid now, but that doesn't mean they can take it for granted. The app is a complex link within an even more complicated structure. The tiniest confusion can lead to full-on miscommunication.

This is why they're worried about the Android app. It's barely been used in practice and never tested intensively. Besides that, Android itself is an unstable platform. Too many manufacturers have added their own tweaks. Over four thousand different kinds of devices run on Android. The point of the concern about the expected or unexpected number of issues is that no issue, big or small, is isolated. Any change or mistake may affect the rest of the code. The more issues, the bigger the delay.

Some of the issues the testers encounter aren't bugs, but choices. After August 2014, everyone switched to IBAN: the eighteen-digit International Bank Account Number. Do you make people fill in the whole number, described somewhere on social media as 'a Frankenstein's monster of letters and numbers that can only have been invented by a human-hating, formula-hugging and possibly psychopathic mind', or just a part? Both create problems.

Marcin, a Polish coder and, like Ali, a Dostoyevsky fan, programs the back-end and Android. He's also the designer of the push, the sending of messages to the user's device. He studied *informatyka* in Warsaw and came to the Netherlands as part of an exchange program. He's the twelfth nationality to join bunq. They now have people from Belgium, Brazil, Canada, Germany, Greece, Hungary, Iceland, Iran, the Netherlands, Poland, Spain and... Italy.

Until recently, Italy was still home to Edoardo, who left the country for love. *Il suo cuore è infranto*, his heart was broken and his body washed up in Amsterdam.

He comes for an interview at bunq for the position of UX designer. User Experience. Orly Square has been struggling with a particular problem for some time: how do you hide your bank balance when you show someone the app?

'Fix it in fifteen minutes and you've got a job,' Ali challenges him.

Edoardo's heart might be broken, but his mind isn't. Within ten minutes he's found the solution. By heart, because his phone battery dies during the interview.

'Payments have to be more personal,' he says, squiggling his design onto paper. Ali nods. Within two minutes he decides to overhaul the back-end of the app and make

Edoardo's solution possible. The Italian can get straight to work. His nickname: 'Parmigiano'.

During the pilot, three whizz kids from the Delft University are asked to spend three months attacking the system non-stop. They go at it like bloodhounds. They find a few bugs, but don't manage to get through security. The app scores high on safety, but, as it turns out, low on accessibility. Especially the payment overview is complicated.

The pilot does bring bunq into a new phase, as Ali announced. 'Front-end, back-end, finance: they're dependent on each other and that creates more and more unity,' HP happily concludes. Those directly involved, and that's nearly everyone, spends day and night and even weekends in touch with each other through a new WhatsApp group named Partysquad. Nearly everyone.

Duke interprets Ali's attitude and his actions as stabs in the back. He sees himself as a founding father, crucial to the company. From, admittedly, day two, he's worked on the development of the concept, given up his career for it, brought in his network, his brother, his best friends, not to mention the potential partners they have so far.

Despite his earlier doubts, his team cracked the license puzzle and now that the countdown to the cursed app-with-no-end finally appears to have begun, he feels like Ali's throwing him out with the trash. He's emotional about it.

Ali's position on the other hand is neither personal nor based on a feeling. It's a conviction, inherent to his character. The cause has to trump everything else, nothing can be allowed to interfere with bunq's progress. Every person thrives in particular situations, is suited to specific tasks. That's when they're at the top of their game. True teamwork entails a razor sharp focus on a common goal that goes beyond individual interests, including Ali's own. It's about the greater good. There's no space for sympathy or friendship in that equation. Those elements are unrelated to what's relevant to bunq. They only apply to personal relationships. Clear and simple.

Ali bears the consequences of his own conviction. If a contract is not renewed, or in case of a premature parting, he's nearly always the one to convey the bad news. He doesn't feel he should place that emotional burden on someone else's shoulders, and after all these years he's become used to being the bad cop.

Mani, 'the crazy motherfucker from Iceland', for example, has been at bunq since 2013. Ali genuinely likes the 27-year-old coder, and he's a true professional. Until his pace and coding accuracy no longer met the changing demands of the programming work. So Mani goes. But they remain friends – until this day they still meet and have fun together.

Ali's attitude towards Duke, although inconvenient given their relationship, is not a matter of personal versus professional. Nor is it a question of loyalty or trust. Even the fact that bunq has become a financial game of Russian roulette for him is not part of the consideration. Ali can't place one individual above the rest. Not principally, nor existentially – not ever.

Andrew, the most experienced businessman, can smell the rot from the sidelines. He's already been skeptical about bunq's commercial progress and now he's noticed a decline in the efforts to find new clients. It's clear to him that internal squabble is preventing a collective outward view.

He can see how the one's expectations no longer match the other's DNA. He thinks Duke is excellent at explaining to new clients what bunq is and what it can do for them, but as a 'manager' in a growing organization, building up a sales team, he's out of his depth. In this case, he mainly sees Ali as the impatient entrepreneur, gunning for instant results.

bunq is now heading towards the fourth phase. Each phase needs the right team: from a start-up team that gets a fledgling organization on its feet, to the permit team that handles the license, to the live team now working on programming and getting ready to deal with the market, to the operational team that needs to be formed as soon as possible and get to work.

Each phase requires its own brand of people and it's often tricky to keep up with a phase change: different capacities are needed, and not everyone has the means to develop those in such a short space of time. Besides: people are creatures of habit, they like stability and predictability — something that bunq, a wildly growing and changing company, cannot offer much of.

During this standoff, Pieter is leaning towards Ali. Their relationship has strengthened since their conflict a few months earlier. Their brief struggle forced them to show their true colors, which ended up bringing them closer together. Pieter accepts Ali as he is — because he realizes Ali has no choice on the matter.

What surprises him is the frequency with which Ali

comes to complain about Duke. Pieter always advises him to talk it over with Duke, after which Ali reports back that they're back on the same page – only to return to Pieter a week or so later. Given that neither Ali nor Duke are tackling the situation head on, Pieter feels as if he'll have to be the one to make a move.

So he does.

'You hold the key,' says Duke in a one-on-one with Pieter.

'If you mean that I agree with you both in terms of the chemistry no longer working,' Pieter responds, 'then I'm afraid you're right.'

He orchestrates a joint meeting with two members of the Supervisory Board. Duke feels isolated in that conversation and has to suppress his anger. His unavoidable departure is *senza amore*, and that influences the atmosphere and everyone's attitude in the difficult conversation.

Yes, Duke's interest in bunq and his role as co-founder are unquestionable. No, they don't find that relevant to the current situation.

On June 9, 2015, Duke's departure from bunq is imminent. Two days later, David, his sales disciple, sits gloomily at the lunch table. Another partner-from-the-start has bailed ahead of the pilot.

Acceleration

The pilot phase places bunq under maximum strain. The coders are back to an average of sixteen-hour workdays, six to seven days a week. The code, having reached over half a million lines, is still being improved, simplified and fixed.

Despite the urge to move forward, bunq can't escape the reality of the slow world around them. Client research has shown that many shops and companies aren't able or willing to work with a purely mobile system yet. After having weighed their options, bunq will have to offer a debit card payment service as well. A bunq debit card comes with a whole new set of system and security demands, plus it requires a DNB stamp of approval. This derails both the pilot and the launch, and they slowly arrive at the idea of a soft launch. One without a card, for now.

Still largely unaware of what's being cooked up at Orly Square, the banking sector is also working feverishly. Within a few years, apparently, they want to 'start executing interpersonal transactions in real-time'. A few years because it requires a completely new infrastructure to be set up in the Netherlands. MasterCard announces a facial recognition trial in the summer of 2015. 'The new generation, which is into selfies ... I think they'll find it cool,' Ajay Bhalla, President of Enterprise Safety and Security tells CNN Money. 'They'll embrace it.'

It's a boiling hot summer. Computers are whirring away in every office, and this time the electricity wires are threatening to melt from the number of fans.

Marketer Marc takes a knife and picks off the glue that holds one of the canteen windows in place. He places suction cups on the glass and he and Ali lift the whole thing out. They do the same to the window on the opposite side, and to one in one of the offices. Classic bunq: if something's not right, fix it.

From the 10th of July onwards, they need to call in a fresh squad of TransIPers to keep the pilot on track. That complicates the management of the and HP is taut with exhaustion and stress. However, most of the bugs they find are solved within minutes. Not hours or days like before. And once fixed, they don't return. The whole thing breathes logic and consistency.

They pass the penetration test. Not even TransIP's top nerds manage to get any closer to cracking the bulletproof glass of bunq's system than the whizz kids from Delft did. Deloitte, by order of DNB, repeats every penetration test once more and asks where bunq bought its system: 'It's the best we've ever seen.' They advise in favor.

No one has any doubt left: in hindsight, the August 2014 rewrite was a stroke of genius.

Launch, anyone?

The testers are thanked kindly in the last week of July. The entire back-end is thinned out once more; dead wood removed and the remnants surgically dismantled. RJ and the others fine-tune the code day and night: delete, delete and rewrite faster. Ali joins them. Once more, everything that received a comment during the pilot phase gets placed under the microscope. Especially their problem child, the faltering facial recognition, the only piece of software bought from an external party...

Sven	Face not recognized. Can't make payments at all. This is complete garbage.	21.45
RJ	You hit the rate limiter.	21.46
Ali	Should have gone for Chinese shit.	21.50
RJ	You can try again Sven.	
21.57		
Sven	Poor lighting was the problem. But these are lighting conditions of average bar.	21.58
Ali	That's why we need voice. Supposedly delivered on July 31st.	22.00
Sven	Signal to noise ratio in crowded bars?	22.01
Ali	Aiming for more than just bars!	22.01

As the coders wrestle with the issue of facial recognition, Geert-Jan manages to develop the debit card infrastructure in no time. He was a decent programmer before joining bunq, but after two years on the frontline, he's truly become an ace.

On the 3rd of August, Ali makes his first test payment with his card at Marnix, a pool in Amsterdam West where he spends 31 minutes, twice a week, swimming fifty-six 25-meter laps. It's a debit card transaction of 4 euros and 10 cents. His video is celebrated grandly in the WhatsApp group. From that moment on, all card transactions are recorded on mobile phones and celebrated like championship finals. For a week. After that the fun wears out and they continue to look to the future.

After the bunq card milestone, DNB lets Pieter know that the 'final decision making process for the conditional permit' has been started. For 'Cards', it's going to take longer: not before the end of August.

Despite what has become deep-rooted impatience, no one mourns. As long as the foundation for the code is still being edited, every minute counts.

Afterparty

Despite the invite-only beta announcement five months ago, it still comes as a surprise to many. Continuous postponement meant many became disillusioned with hope. But this time the invitations are actually sent out on time — the 9th of September.

The official, but limited, public launch is in one week, on Djoeri's birthday. Exactly two years after his arrival at bunq and exactly one year and one day after they received their banking license.

The software is still 'a work in progress', but the app is good enough to function and be tested in practice. The cap on the number of users serves as a realistic preparation for an unlimited number of customers, without losing control. The limit is set where the number of bugs or problems are representative, yet controllable.

They don't know how long the beta test will last. It depends on the feedback and reported bugs. It's not even certain whether the system will continue to work. The app's never had to deal with more than four users at a time.

The Support Team is scaled up. It has to be fully operational from day one: every user must be able to contact bunq directly. That's why HR has already been expanded. bunq will have to grow super fast, or all efforts will have been in vain. They've had such a massive influx of new employees over the past few weeks that Roos has had to chase the supplier for more laptops in less time.

Just as nature sometimes gives off warning signs before

impending catastrophes, the Orly Square office makes it clear that it's unwilling to suck up any more expansions and expected growth. There's a water leak in the canteen, concrete decay in the parking garage, mice in the offices and the elevator increasingly has a mind of its own.

With the date set, Team IT goes into overdrive, backed up by two TransIPers: Reinier, who's worked for bunq before, and Ryan. Ryan proudly wears the same printed T-shirt every day: 'Ryan is a boss. It's true. Ali says so.'

Not everything is functioning as it should. Debit card payments regularly fail and sometimes money gets stuck in an in-between-transfer account. Bills are inconsistent with the number of transactions, facial recognition is unstable, the automatic testing system keeps malfunctioning, system management's faltering and the Android app is showing signs of trouble.

But, hey. The first iPhone had a one-hour battery life. Nothing is ever perfect, at some point you just have to run with it. Besides, the iOS app is running smoothly and the back-end is perfectly stable.

The location for the invite-only is half a mile east of the office, in the same industrial terrain in a warehouse belonging to The Datacenter Group. Comparable to other datacenters, it's a well secured vault, which bunq makes use of. The warehouse location is not only practical, but also symbolic: bunq's not a bank, but an IT start-up, down to the bone.

On the morning of the invite-only, Djoeri, Anne and Stini disappear into the warehouse with large black screens to mask endless racks of building materials, tools and computer parts. They cordon off an area and fill it with folding chairs, sofas and high tables, positioned in a semi-circle around a raised stage. A little further along, they will have a bar and a few portable toilets.

For the first time, Ali will be giving a one-man show, albeit reluctantly. Neither Pieter nor Djoeri nor any other bunqer was up for it, or felt it was right to be standing up there beside him. Ali has them remove the elevated stage: bunq is on the same level as the people, not above them.

A final set of hurdles has to be overcome. There's Ali's usual nerves for public speaking, but even more so his reluctance to lose the last of his anonymity. He fears that going up there alone will link bunq too much to him as a person. And it should never be about the person.

Ali's performance will be filmed and sent out as a press release. Pieter, 'The Slooth', is directing the test recording. At the last minute, he asks marketer Marc to operate the slides they'll be projecting onto the back wall. They have to switch back and forth between these slides – showing the bunq logo, for example – and live footage of Ali's phone. The slides have to be swiped in the right direction at the right moment on the Mac. The slide order turns out to be a mess. Marc adapts a few colors and then all he has to focus on that evening is the timing and the swipe-direction.

Ali's dress rehearsal is practically flawless, but it takes a lot out of him. He may have recovered slightly from his head injury, but not fully. His memory often fails him. Insomnia undermines his days and weigh him down with pessimism and bitterness. What he lost in brain cells will never regenerate, the doctors told him. He is, however, forging new connections in his brain through training. He's managing to break up his chronic fatigue and lethargy with moments of his former sharpness and spark. He manages to tune into that sharpness during the dress rehearsal, but it takes an incredible amount of energy. With eight hours to go, Ali drags himself home to get some sleep.

On a rainy Tuesday evening, on September 15, 2015, the first guests make their way across the wet parking lot. At 8:15 pm, to everyone's relief, the hall fills up. There's even a line at the bar. At 8:25, the guests are invited to take their seats. Every chair is taken and many have to stand. Lights dim at exactly 8:30. The bunqers start off a loud round of applause, and are joined by the rest.

Ali's excited, nervous, happy. Over two hundred people. It's way more than he'd anticipated. He walks in through the audience and greets them by announcing: 'An extraordinary day!'

When he walks on, he notices a pillow on the floor. Johan, Robbert and Andreas got it for him as a surprise gift. An image of Scrooge McDuck is printed onto the pillow, sitting on a bag of money, with the caption: 'Finally finished. Now get some sleep! The bros.'

Ali utters a Freudian slip as he passes the pillow to Djoeri for safekeeping: 'Hold me'.

He paces back and forth, collects his thoughts and regains control of himself and his speech. He secretly learned it by heart. A condensed version of the non-stop flood of emotions and events of the past years.

Then... *Hammer time!*

'What I long for, what I live for, is the creation of new things. Making something out of nothing,' he begins, in English. The only language he's wanted to be addressed in over the past few days. To practice for this event.

His hesitance disappears, he starts to talk more quickly.

He recalls how the idea of bunq sprung up: the financial crisis, outdated banks, unwanted products, IT as a way of providing the service people do want. If your customers like what you do, you do well. If not, you don't. So: a company based on a service model. But not a bank.

Ali: 'Ask any bunqer what we are, and they will always answer: We're an...'

bunqers: 'IT-company-with-a-banking-license!'

Ali races through the past four years, starting with a few adventurers in an empty building that hadn't been cleaned or heated for winters on end, trying to attain a greenfield banking license. From the afternoon off to celebrate their conditional offer – first round of applause – he steams on ahead to how they experimented and built prototypes. As quickly as possible, to get to the live on-screen demonstration of what they built in a single year, at 'ludicrous speed': a one-hundred percent mobile payment platform. Everything real-time, beautiful, attractive, easy to use.

Out of view, Esan and company are ready to step in if anything fails. Ever since a German fellow bunqer returned to his *Heimat* a few weeks ago, Esan is the only DevOps member. That makes him software developer as well as person responsible for the functioning of the network and servers. Including right now.

But there's no need to step in. Ali's demo proceeds flawlessly. The world's first mobile payment from person to person instead of account to account. As Edoardo, the UX designer, put it during his first week at bunq: 'It works without a glitch'.

In all its smoothness, it looks so deceptively simple that Ali has to subtly hint to the audience that this is worthy of applause.

With each new feature he reveals, the audience is more and more impressed.

Registering the mobile, sharing and adding accounts, NearPay, requesting a debit card.. It all goes to plan – including facial recognition, even at low-light levels.

Two swanky videos display bunq's strong social function and Ali asks the audience to sign up and become the latest test group – after all, that's why they were invited.

Ali calls out: 'Where are the magical people that call themselves bunqers? bunqers, please come on up!'

Accompanied by loud cheers, they join in front of the bunq logo. Ali thanks them for all of these months, these years of work.

'I know I'm not an easy guy. But just look at what we've done together! We've accomplished something amazing, something incredible. Many were convinced we'd never pull it off. And look where we are now!'

Then: 'So you can tell the story to your grandchildren some day, we have something for you. Something to help others recognize a bunqer. Roos?'

They all get a T-shirt with the words 'First 50 bunqers' printed across it.

A thunderous round of applause echoes around the room.

At the bar, veteran Jordi is chatting to David. Sergey's here, as are Mani, Amir, Jan de Ruiter, Jeroen Kremers... the latter two dressed in suits, unlike everyone else.

Arthur Docters van Leeuwen is sorely missed. Shortly before the start of the event, he sent a heart-warming message to Ali, explaining that he was unwell and would have to cancel.

Emiel Roozen also sent a message to congratulate them. The reason DNB didn't invite the board member-to-be for a review at the time has become largely public knowledge.

On July 2, 2012, DNB implemented a set nominal interest rate for long-term insurance obligations. Soon after, they received an anonymous tip that a large company, Delta Lloyd, had allegedly sold part of its interest protection just before the implementation of the interest rate. DNB suspected that this could be classed as insider trading. Although he was not the guilty party, financial director Roozen took the hit, and took the blame in the media too.

Many new bunqers don't know the old ones, and vice versa. That is certainly not the case for two super coders, Jesper and Sven. Jesper, 'Boy Genius', chose to do a postdoc in Berlin after exactly one year at bunq. Something to do with quantum mechanics. Sven, who joined at the end of 2014, decided to return to Utrecht to finish his studies, in doing so preventing a penalty of a massive college debt. Now, just for this moment, they've reunited with the bunqers that stayed.

A few tables down, Duke is talking to Andrew, or 'Lemon' as the bunqers call him. His decision to attend came as naturally as his invitation, although he did have to overcome a hurdle or two to be there. For him the event is overshadowed by a feeling of loss and disappointment. He's angry, and he mainly blames Ali personally. He has no interest in becoming a bunq customer and doesn't sign up. Many of his former colleagues in turn take offense to this attitude.

HP and colleagues are ready with their laptops for anyone who wants to get onboard on the spot. The majority of guests walk over and download the app there and then to take part in the 'invite only beta-test'.

As of this evening the non-disclosure agreement is void for nearly everything, with the exception of a few extra applications bunq is still hatching out. Paul van Liempt can finally announce to the world what 'Project X' entails.

Just after 1 am, the last of the diehards have left and they can turn the lights on. The Datacenter warehouse is locked.

Djoeri, The Slooth and Edoardo left the party a few hours before. The three of them and Ali sit down at bunq to edit the video and get it online and to the press asap.

At 01:18, just as Marc dives into bed, the WhatsApp Partysquad beeps.

Ali is short of grawlixes, a typographic cartoon idiom, to express his frustration.

'@#$%&! up with the logos. @#$%&! @#$%&! @#$%&!'

Marc asks what's going on.

'So we can't use any of the @#$%&! Video. What a @#$%&! @#$%&! mess...'

It goes quiet for hours, while the men in Orly Square toil on sleeplessly. At 07:05 am, Ali reports back and sends a message via the app that the website will not be going live anytime soon, and they're not to be interrupted until further notice. Any press should be directly put through to him. He finishes with 'good night'.

When Marc arrives at the office, shortly after, he understands the commotion. On the video, their partners' logos are constantly being displayed in the background. That slide should have been replaced with a similar one without the logos as Ali walked on. During the presentation itself, no one had noticed. Everyone was so focused on Ali's performance.

It also turns out that one of the cameras went to standby for seven minutes: a third of the presentation. Frame by frame correction is the only solution. The demos of the app that appeared on the big screen will have to be 'acted out', timed perfectly and slotted into the running video.

Djoeri, Parmigiano and The Slooth work for forty near-uninterrupted hours, until they literally can't speak from lack of sleep, let alone work.

Friday, at midnight, the new video finally goes live. It's been a slightly different afterparty than they'd imagined.

'We're live!'

Unexpectedly soon – within a week – the 'onboarding' of new users comes to a halt. The number of iOS users has reached its limit. An enormous amount of feedback, questions and suggestions is fired at bunq. To be able to provide an immediate reaction, all bunqers are given customer support training, including the two members of the Board of Directors: Ali and Pieter.

Many questions are operational in nature, concerning failed debit card payments, for example, but some are more existential in nature: what makes bunq truly different?

'We've been so close to our product for so long that we have to re-learn how to explain what the app actually is and what it does,' The Slooth explains to his class. 'It's a trap: we know the app we built through and through. To others, it's just an app: so what? We'll have to be able to explain the difference, referring to things people know, like other payment apps.'

But is bunq really so revolutionary and different compared to other payment apps? According to the betas, it looks fresher and it's more fun and easier to use. It allows for direct, purely mobile user-to-user transactions and that's unique. Nevertheless, all Dutch banks are trying to make their apps more user friendly now. bunq has to realize it's putting a 1.0 version up against the umpteenth release of existing payment apps.

Is the fact that they want to change the way the financial world works, the fact that they're chipping away at the foundations of 'too big to fail', enough of a reason to choose bunq? For some, yes. For most, no. The question that counts is 'what can I do with it?'

The revolutionary difference between bunq and other payment apps in terms of use is in the very near future. Part of their raison d'être is the fact that they can keep up with the needs of their users as an IT company (with a banking license). Even be ahead of the curve where possible. Small, flexible companies like theirs can theoretically develop and grow their product at the speed of light.

On the one hand, there's no limit to development, or how user-friendly they can be. For a lot of apps, people are quick to ask 'is this all? Why won't it do this?'. On the other hand, if an app offers functions the users haven't (yet) asked for, no one will use them.

In practice, people's ability to imagine something is based on, and therefore limited by, the payment apps they know. Are people able to imagine a network that goes beyond national borders, in which the whole world can be directly financially/socially interconnected? Are they able to conceive of an AppleTV for finance? It comes down to this: the greater the users' imagination, the faster and more revolutionary bunq app's developments.

At the top of the betas' wish list is a chat function. Nearly everyone asks for it. Just sending money, however quick and easy, is too sterile without communication.

'Connect' is born from an idea Roos has during a round of grocery shopping. Ali asks her to bring a few personal items for him.

'How useful would it be if I could hook my card up to your account,' says Roos.

'Genius,' answers Ali. 'Allowing someone to access a limited amount of money for a limited amount of time, just using their own bunq card...'

And thus 'Connect' is born: the real-time creation of group bank accounts, shared with one, two or many others – even an entire football team. Ali suddenly sees a use for the symbol he visualized months ago in his slumber: two linked, abstract hands.

The amount of unique comments from the test group starts to decrease within a few weeks. bunq prepares for the inevitable moment they go live with the inevitable growth spurt that'll come with it, and scales up support even further.

The office space they moved into 'with an eye to the future' is starting to get very tight in places. The walls of the offices are bursting at the seams. Even the storage space is now a place of work, in among the boxes of cartridges and printing paper. Holding a meeting in a quiet corner is no longer an option.

'Let's go to your car,' Pieter suggests when he wants to talk about something with Ali. They descend into the decaying concrete basement garage, like they're about to discuss something very shifty.

On a Friday evening, during the roundup of the working week and the start of the working weekend, Ali gives his usual status update on what's to be done and by whom.

'This is the final call. If you can't make a deadline, this is your last chance to say so. Nobody? Good. It's a go! We launch in two weeks!'

The bunqers are completely overwhelmed. Two weeks!

That's only about three hundred hours until they launch the public beta, when they roll out the not-quite-finished product to the masses.

Three hundred hours for Andreas, Menno, Petros, RJ and all the others to make the code shockproof. Once bunq is live, it'll grow with a massive bang.

All bunqers have to get to work. 110 hours a week, day and night.

And they do. They work their asses off, again. For the first few days, they're full of fire and enthusiasm, everything and everyone gunning for that one day.

After a full week, a clean 24/7, the killing pace takes its toll. Bugs pop up and drive Team Android to despair. There's still so much that can go wrong...

Combined with stress and lack of sleep, that notion breaks them up. A bit of extra sleep? Not possible if you spend those few hours with your eyes wide open with worry. New people come in and need to be trained, but by whom and where? When?

bunq is hurtling towards the three-hundred-hour limit, inevitably and mercilessly, like a high-speed train without an emergency break. The seventy-two hours before the launch are melded into flow. The Slooth and his team, fueled by Red Bull, lay the final touches to the promo videos. Ali rehearses his new keynote like a long, long mantra.

Then, at 07:45 am, after two weeks and one night of work, the sun rises for the last time. It's the final sunrise before the launch, vaguely visible behind the gray curtains.

bunq races straight through this checkpoint too.

On November 24, 2015, the day of the launch, they have

the exact same scenario in place as ten weeks before at the invite-only. The main assignment is also the same: tonight, nothing can go wrong.

The location and the elements repeat themselves: puddles of rain glisten in the artificial light on the parking lot of The Datacenter warehouse.

Unlike the invite-only, this public beta is attended by the press. The national news channel has indicated at the last minute that they'd like to interview Ali before he goes on. bunq has also hired a camera crew. They want to avoid the mayhem they had with the videos last time, at any expense.

7.45 pm: Rain.
8.15 pm: The audience fills the Warehouse.
8.25 pm: The guests find a seat. Room is fully filled yet again.
8:30 pm: Lights fade. Applause.

Ali comes on. Again, he's 'super nervous', enthused and excited. A similar positive tension buzzes around the audience. The atmosphere sizzles with anticipation.

'Continuing to move forward and improving, that's the essence of bunq,' Ali begins. 'bunq is about what you actually enjoy and want to use. We've already received 284 ideas for improvement and feature requests. The question we've heard the most? He gestures his hands towards the audience: 'How do I invite my friends to bunq!'

His thirty-minute keynote is about the future and barely touches on the past, unlike his speech at the invite-only. He thanks Roos for 'connect', and a video shows how it works. Then the second-most popular feature request follows. Ali explains the functionality, how you can send each other messages and pictures, texts. 'And we call it... chat!', he jokes, successfully.

Nearly every sentence, every image in the presentation shows something new, something unprecedented, and promises more to come. Then, after almost thirty meaningful minutes and an eager applause, a page-long code appears on the screen. It's the activation code to make the app go live.

Ali walks over to a laptop set up in advance, finishes a line, activates the program, enters a password, and...

'*We're live!*' The three historic words flash across the screen.

Confetti is blown from cannons, the music starts and the bunqers explode in euphoria. This is new, this is now, this is the future!

And for the first time in ages, overwhelmed by the moment, Ali can't get enough of the volume.

Nrc.nl, a Dutch newspaper, posts a positive article straight after the confetti drops. *Bunq: WhatsApp for banks*. At the same time the article voices some doubt: 'Whether people will actually go to the effort of installing and using the app remains to be seen'.

The bunqers throw themselves at the video editing, anxious to avoid a repeat of what happened last time. In one night and a morning, it's finished. After a brief slumber, they take one more look. All done.

Un-showered, but with a full half hour of rest behind him, Ali drives to the studio of 'De Wereld Draait Door', a popular primetime live talk show. The editor has asked him to arrive a little ahead of time, so that he feels more comfortable during the broadcast.

As soon as the live broadcast starts, he walks over to the guest table – too early, because the broadcast hasn't started yet. Ali sits down among the audience. The live music's good, but so very loud that he bites his lip to fight the pain. As he wipes his sweaty palms on his pants, presenter Matthijs van Nieuwkerk gives him a fatherly nod. That calms his nerves and he's grateful for Matthijs' empathy.

At the table, he's joined by Jeroen Smit, investigative reporter and author of bestselling book *The Perfect Prey*, about how ABN Amro was led astray by the arrogance and blind ambition of its top executives.

Smit is well-prepared: he visited bunq's launch as well as ABN Amro's IPO, both in the same week. During the introduction, he explains that the difference could not have been greater and that bankers are scared to death of the internet. Because internet kills the middleman, and a banker is little more than that.

Visibly enjoying his words, Ali nods at his neighbor approvingly. His only concern is that he has to leave his iPhone off for the duration of the show.

In front of the cameras Ali notes that three teams are already working round the clock to cope with the flow of new users. He neglects to mention that the list mainly consists of the many that were left out because of the cap on the private beta. And of course yesterday's guests.

The last update he saw on Partysquad was 'only 20 pending users left'. He's unreachable for bunq, so he has no idea of the current status.

The show is followed by the eight o'clock news, which also provides bunq with ample coverage, including a short fragment of their interview with Ali. Other media pick up on the story too.

That's when it happens. Their twenty pending users shoots up to two thousand pending users.

A dozen bunqers work through the evening and decide to go for an all-nighter. It's onboarding at Mach-speed. By morning, they're counting 1,190 pending users, by the afternoon it's 1,250 again. bunq is trending as number 1 in the app store.

HP calls for help from the Partysquad:

HP	Everybody who can assist with onboarding GoGoGo!!!!	19:47
HP	Can someone bring some deodorant tomorrow for a nice classic deodorant-shower? And a toothbrush...	03:27
Ali	Please be as silent as possible tomorrow morning. Multiple colleagues are sleeping in different rooms	05.06
Dineke	Anyone need anything?	08:29
Marc	Sleep	08:49

The bunqers can't handle it alone. They call in friends for help. Ten new temps familiarize themselves with the validation of potential new clients and answering their questions. Support is also tasked to train up a few new workers at top speed.

On day three, Guido and Carmen — who have been working in back-office and HR respectively for six months or so – guide twenty flex workers into the building. Every trained bunqer takes two to three friends or flex workers under their wing. The canteen's overflowing, the ping-pong table folded away in the corner.

Acceptance, conversation, transactions: it's all real-time. The admin, the system that interacts with the client, is groaning under the strain. There are so many people working on it at the same time that it's become painfully slow. There are not enough IBANs to go around. Equens assigns them, but because of the possibility of opening ten different accounts – another new feature – they soon run out. They'll have to wait for new ones. The SMS gateway, the system that sends messages to verify clients' phone numbers, is threatening to buckle under the overload. The backend is creaking, but holding up.

Again, work continues through the night. They've booked rooms in a nearby hotel, but most end up taking quick naps in the corridor or under a desk. Active sleepers keep setting off the sensitive motion sensors.

On Friday at 2:15 pm, bunq reaches the 10,000-user milestone. After that, the users continue to pour in, but at 4:30 pm, for a short moment, they have precisely '0' pending users.

Stop the clock!

Because at exactly that moment, at 4:30 in the afternoon, during that milestone, it dawns on Ali that they're no longer a start-up, but a company with clients.

For a split-second only, his onboarding fingers still resting on the keys, he's overcome by reality. It's a feeling of grandeur and irrelevance, triumph and loss. And a little melancholy. The efforts, the worry, the sleepless nights and the lost friendships: was it worth the years and the sacrifice?

As soon as the number of pending users changes, Ali's fingers and mind fall back into a natural gear. No time to stop and think. No time to hold back.

Every moment is a link to the next phase. bunq has to grow as soon as possible, from individual to business, from the Netherlands to abroad. The app has to be better and more fun. Even better, even more fun.

bunq wants a change in paradigm. To break free from banks. People have to have the freedom of choice again. To regain power over their money.

And onwards!

I'm Going to Start a Bank

'Don't tell anyone,' said Ali. 'I'm going to start a bank...'

That was in 2012, at the height of the financial crisis. Since then, he's surrounded himself with young, driven people, preferably straight from university. Even including Pieter's gray hairs the average age is a mere 27 years. He enticed them all, not with money, but with the promise of changing the world. On starting a new kind of bank together, a bank existing only of an app and a server. A bank without bonuses or historical ballast, without a tainted culture. A bank with a clean slate.

At a dizzying pace, they took an unforgettable and initially blind ride on a roller coaster. They tried a lot, they failed a lot. The peaks and valleys were equal in height and depth, and the turns were sharp and unexpected. None of them knew where and when the project would end, not even Ali. Everything was personal, everything was business, everything was at stake. The idea was simple, the execution seemed impossible. And that's where the fun begins.

bunq has met every legal condition required to get a full banking license. Not to bank in the traditional sense of the word, but a license to do things differently. Ask a bunqer what they are and they will answer: 'An IT company with a banking license.'

bunq's revenue model isn't based on acquired funds, but on customer satisfaction and service. Soon after the start of the pilot, and after some twenty-five variants, the subscription model has finally been set. bunq basically makes money from their corporate clients.

In contrast to 2012, bunq no longer revolts against the existing financial world and its structures. They're a little mouse that roars like a lion, but not the anti-bank. They simply consider traditional banks to be a thing of the past. In terms of that anti-bank attitude, times have changed, too. Banks are no longer the largest threat to welfare and stability in the media. That position seems to have been taken over by international terrorism.

bunq is now looking for its own place and support network, its own friends. Free of the charged word 'bank', they expect to appeal mainly to young, unburdened people, free of prejudice against the new and the changing. Those who can distinguish between new and imitation and true from false. They will co-create their new services with them. Services that exist alongside the traditional banks' products. Services that better meet real-time needs than the existing ones. Services that will continue to grow and be a constant seed for everything that can be faster, better or more beautiful.

Change is slow and not everyone will embrace or even understand it. It will be visible in new, independent parties applying for banking licenses. It's reflected in the behavior of big banks, as they increasingly feel the disruptive pressure of newcomers and the demand for services from their clients. Big banks who will disguise their own apps in faux leather every time bunq or someone else comes up with a real innovation. It will be reflected in the growth and development of bunq itself. To quote Jeroen Smit, it's 'shifting innovation'. It begins small, but it eats its way in.

Banks have neither the culture nor the flexibility to

change with the times and end the way they go about money. It will be an endless struggle within the larger banks to open up windows of thought and let fresh air into the smoky backrooms of their bankers, the middlemen.

As per April 1, 2016, bunq has moved a few hundred meters south to a larger office. From the Orly Square canteen, you could already see 'das bunq'r'. As usual, the bunqers work day and night and Ali still demands the impossible. Not only from them, but also from himself.

Every now and then he meets up with Jordi, who has continued to climb the steep career path, stretching beyond the peaks of Mount Olympus, and who is currently working in a senior-legal-counsel-regulatory-affairs-and-securities-law-like job at NN Group. And Duke? Or Attila, Long, Peter, Sergey and all those other Clearians and bunqers who were there from the start? No need for concern there. If you can handle bunq, you can handle the world.

bunq is live and growing, emerging and developing further, far beyond existing borders and lovingly going against all odds.

But that's another chapter.

FAST FORWARD...

The unicorn

From a revolutionary idea for mobile banking to an international community with millions of users in thirty European countries. A lot can happen in ten years: A pocket-sized service organization, born out of frustration with existing major banks, their lack of service and their focus on money, went on to change the way these major banks work. And we're talking about very fundamental changes here: payment requests with your mobile, direct payments, QR codes: where bunq innovated, traditional banks had to play catch-up. Or rather, they tried to.

bunq was the first ever bank with a subscription-based business model, completely and totally focused on the user. At its launch on November 24, 2015, it was already a technological and ideological trailblazer, and it's been introducing game-changing innovations at lightning speed ever since. Success followed just as quickly. Year after year, user deposits doubled, and even during COVID bunq's growth was unstoppable. Not bad for 'a pack of pups who relentlessly hounded their dreams into reality'.

This rapid growth came with a hefty price tag though: six million euros, seventeen million euros, seventy million euros... The one number that didn't go up was the number of investors: Ali remained bunq's sole benefactor. The result? bunq remained free and independent and could do as it saw fit.

'I'd rather sell a kidney than look for an investor!' Ali famously said once, even though his dream was costing him about fifty-seven euros a minute (!) at one point. Not a problem: as long as bunq's growth was on track, making it to break-even was just a matter of time, time TransIP continued to pay for with its excellent financial results.

bunq employees were equally optimistic: *whatever happens, in the end we will prevail.* Until that day, everyone knew, they were the underdog, free of any blame and pure of heart. Success was inevitable...

And so bunq grew relentlessly day after day. It launched abroad, in Germany, Austria, France, Spain, up to 30 countries in total. It expanded its product with all kinds of new and exciting features and gradually found a balance with subscription fees and interest income.

Fast forward to 2020, exactly five years after bunq's launch: many hundreds of millions of euros in deposits are safely kept at the European Central Bank (ECB). Safe, sure, but also very expensive: with the ECB's negative interest rate policy bunq has to pay about 0.8% over all those hundreds of millions every month. These are giant losses that bunq needs to make up for itself.

In short: almost break-even, but not quite...

bunq calls upon some longtime advisors, people who also assisted TransIP in the past. The result is a delightfully simple idea: take the money stored at the ECB – it's not doing anything anyway – and do something good with it that is as safe and responsible as possible. That way bunq mitigates the negative interest rate losses and empowers its users to do good with their money. Points for creativity, but how to turn such an idea into reality?

Enter Pollen Street Capital: a private equity fund

specializing in asset management and credit strategies, accelerating the progress of financial and business service industries.

And who just happens to be one of the biggest accelerators of the last five years? Exactly: bunq!

With Pollen Street's capital, bunq can shift gears to even faster growth through mergers and acquisitions. So it can reach more people and make a bigger impact. So it can do what's right.

And what about that kidney Ali would sell before welcoming outside investors? That kidney hasn't gone anywhere, nor will it. An investor that helps you grow, one that buys a mere ten percent stake of a successful challenger bank for a hundred and seventy million euros - indeed, this is now the going rate for this 'pack of pups' - is very different from an investor that helps you survive.

TransIP bought Ali time. With Pollen Street, bunq has gained it. Moreover, Ali puts in another twenty-five million of his own money, on top of the hundred million he invested in bunq over the past five years.

Shifting gears through mergers and acquisitions... Sounds great on paper, but the reality of it presents itself in the acquisition of Capitalflow, a lending company based in Dublin, Ireland.

Capitalflow could easily be considered a sister company of bunq: it provides credit to the Irish community through a digital platform, to local entrepreneurs, transport companies, builders, landlords... Like bunq, it's forged and maintained a very close relationship with its community and, unsurprisingly, shares the same key value: "users first".

If bunq and Capitalflow join forces, Capitalflow could leverage the money bunq stores at the ECB to help its customers, while bunq in return gets a fee on these deposits from Capitalflow, instead of paying fees to the ECB. Win-win. Brilliant in its simplicity.

A magical moment: in April 2021, bunq surpasses €1 billion euros in user deposits. Shortly thereafter, in July 2021, the company celebrates its first ever profitable month, a prelude of things to come: fundamental profitability, free of financial worry.

With bunq being in the best shape it's ever been in, acquiring Capitalflow quickly becomes a no-brainer for everyone involved. It's a game-changing deal one could confidently submit to DNB for approval.

Although...

DNB remains traditionally strict, especially with a deal of this size, requiring many regulatory checks and investigations, and not just on bunq's end. Capitalflow is even younger than bunq and hails from Ireland, which was one of the worst affected countries during the last crisis... would any of this factor into DNB's assessment?

Interest advantages, securities, future growth: bunq has no shortage of good arguments, and ample documentation to back these up. Months of paperwork and consultations ensue, with the legal deadline of ninety days upping the pressure with each and every passing second.

Then, seemingly out of the blue: 'Our country gains another unicorn,' *Quote,* the Dutch magazine on business, money and career, headlines enthusiastically.

And just like that, it's official! bunq is an independent,

self-financed Dutch unicorn valued at a staggering 1.6 billion euros. Fueled with ambition, bent on writing history.

> At this point Ali Niknam can best be described as a Unicorn Whisperer. Thanks to a private equity deal (...) bunq was instantly valued at €1.6 billion. This makes the online bank the third company Niknam (co-)founded valued at more than a billion and thus obtaining the unicorn status so heavily coveted among startups.
>
> *Quote*, Martijn Zeven (01/12/2021)

It's a historical, unprecedented achievement by a pack of pups. bunq, the young challenger, is full of pride and ready for the future: bank of The Free!

Justification

At the beginning of 2012, Ali asked me to write the story of his start-up. He wanted to document the events, so that he and everyone who felt the need, could look back on the process in hindsight, regardless of the outcome. He was sure it would take no more than six months.

The birth of bunq took at least six times as long. Partly because of that, more has remained unsaid than has been described, and not all of those to whom bunq owes its existence have ended up in the book. People who are in the book have been based on my observations and typing. To anyone who feels offended, flattered, ignored or embarrassed: my apologies.

After signing the non-disclosure agreement, I spent many Thursdays at bunq. Ali and I were already friends and I became fond of those he surrounded himself with. Those who formed the heart and soul of bunq: Anne, Carmen, Duke, Daan, David, Djoeri, Dominik, Guido, HP, Marc, Petros, Pieter, Roos, Stini, Thijs...

It's clear that I am no impartial outsider. And even if I had been, the bunqers' effort, fire and enthusiasm would undoubtedly have infected me. My own distrust towards banks remains the same as ever, but the bunqers have made me believe that the sector can change — thanks to banks other than the existing ones.

During my visits, I was free to speak to anyone and only sporadically encountered an oath of secrecy, mostly regarding conversations with DNB. The manuscript was read by Ali and Pieter, so as not to infringe on common confidentiality within the financial world, and partly by Arthur Docters van Leeuwen regarding literal quotes. Finally, Toon van de Put came in to polish the rougher edges.

In lieu of full financial disclosure, I think it right to reveal the incentives I've received for this project. For what amounts to four years of sporadic work, I received a total sum of 15,000 euros. Although I haven't actually checked, I estimate a total of 3,000 euros in travel costs. My lunches at bunq were always free and at the end of 2014 I received a Christmas gift: an Xbox One with two controllers and 'Call of Duty: Advanced Warfare', in which I have managed to get to level 50. During the writing process I was also granted the right to publication by Kompas Publishers.

The following sentences, straight from Ali's mouth, have remained unchanged throughout each year and each edit, as has their value: 'Realistic expectations lead to realistic results. But realism doesn't change the world, only dreams do.'

And I was there to witness them.

Siebe Huizinga

Timeline

Founding of Game Changers B.V.	March 26, 2012
Lunch Ali and Duke	July 19, 2012
ProjectClear.nl	February 6, 2013
Visit Arthur Docters van Leeuwen	February 15, 2013
First meeting with DNB	June 13, 2013
Bright becomes bunq	July 23, 2013
Conceptual application to DNB	August 3, 2013
Reaction DNB	September 27, 2013
Final application to DNB	November 26, 2013
DNB expresses doubts	January 3, 2014
Triple media exposure	May 7, 2014
Review at DNB	June 13, 2014
Demonstration of the app at DNB	July 8, 2014
Financing final	September 5, 2014
Permit from DNB	September 16, 2014
Launch and test phase postponed	December 12, 2014
Start test phase	April 13, 2015
Invite-only beta	September 16, 2015
Launch	November 24, 2015
Expansion to Germany and Austria	March 9, 2017
Launch across the EU, Norway, Iceland	October 1, 2019
bunq becomes officially a unicorn	December 2, 2021

Index

G

H

I

K

L

M

T

U

V

W

Y

Z